Richard Wurmbrand

Titles in *Heroes of the Cross* series

Forthcoming titles in this series

RICHARD WURMBRAND

The Man Who Came Back

by
Mary Drewery

Marshall Pickering

Marshall Morgan and Scott
Marshall Pickering
1 Beggarwood Lane, Basingstoke, Hants, RG23 7LP UK.

ISBN 0 551 01039 8

Printed in Great Britain by
Cox & Wyman Ltd, Reading, Berks.

Contents

POLAND

USSR

CZECHOSLOVAKIA

AUSTRIA HUNGARY

YUGOSLAVIA

ITALY

ALBANIA GREECE

BULGARIA

TURKEY

HUNGARY

Gherla

Cluj

TRANSYLVANIA

Sibiu

YUGOSLAVIA

CARPA

Orsova

Cralova

R. Danube

PRE-WORLD WAR II BOUNDARY ••••••••

LAND OVER 3,000 FEET

LAND CEDED TO RUSSIA

LAND CEDED TO BULGARIA

0   50 Miles

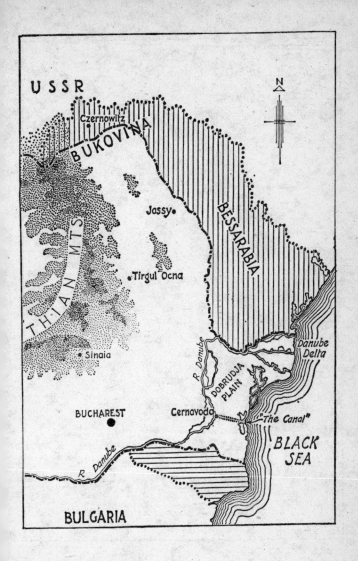

Prologue

WINTER IS A bitter season in Bucharest. The *crivaţ*, a frost-hard wind from the north-east, blows down across the plains from Siberia bringing gnawing cold to Rumania's capital. The streets are mantled in snow; the string of lakes round the city's northern perimeter gleam dully like pewter under their coating of ice.

That Sunday in 1948, however, had a feel in the air of coming spring. The wind had eased a little. The sun shone, gilding the snow on the branches of the trees till it slid in a wet spray on to the pavement beneath. It was February 29th – Leap Year Day. An extra day. A once-in-four-year bonus. So it was fitting that it was a Sunday and that one could give thanks to God for twenty-four additional hours to spend in His service.

There were no people about. Even had church-going not been discouraged under the Communist régime, the streets would still have been quiet at that hour for the man was early.

'I'll see you in half an hour or so,' he had told his wife as he left home. 'I've a number of things to see to before church. I've a wedding this afternoon.'

So the man strode purposefully over the hard-packed snow, long legs moving with the easy confidence of one who enjoys his work, deep-set eyes alive to the promise of the day.

The car came up so fast behind him that he did not hear its approach. Only as it pulled up alongside with a squeal of brakes and a spray of churned up snow did he notice that it was a Ford—a big Ford, black and sinister. The doors opened and two men sprang out, seizing the man from either side and twisting his arms up behind him till he was forced to double up with the pain. He was thrust roughly into the rear seat of the Ford and his kidnappers piled in with him. A third man had moved round to the front and, when the victim at last managed to straighten up, he found himself looking down the barrel of a revolver levelled at him over the back of the seat. A fourth man was at the wheel, the engine still ticking over.

The car slid into gear, gathered speed and drew away. Only the skid-marks made by the tyres and a patch of churned-up snow indicated that anything had disturbed the sabbath peace of that winter morning.

Inside the car, no-one spoke.

The man struggled to collect his thoughts. Now that the first shock of the attack was over, his keen brain sought to assess his situation. Strangely, he felt no fear. He had been expecting this arrest and his mind was prepared to meet it. The Police had imprisoned him before, so he knew what to expect, what questions they would ask.

But what of Sabina, his wife? What of his little son, Mihai? Would they guess what had become of him? He drove personal thoughts out of his mind and sought to concentrate on preparing himself for the coming ordeal.

The car sped along the wide boulevards. There was more traffic as they approached the city centre. Through the car window, the man glimpsed a plaque on a wall giving the name of the street: *Calea Rahovei*. That, he knew, was where the Communist Secret Police had their headquarters and, as if in confirmation, the car slowed down, turned in through large steel gates and stopped. The gates clanged shut.

'Out!' said one of the kidnappers, and the man was bundled unceremoniously from the car and into a bare office. An official was seated behind a desk. He motioned to the kidnappers who began, swiftly and expertly, to empty their victim's pockets. Wallet, identity papers, money, pen, keys, handkerchief. All were placed on the desk.

'Take off your tie,' said the official.

The prisoner did so, and laid it beside his possessions on the desk.

'Now your shoe-laces.'

The man removed those, too, and laid them beside his tie. The official, flicking through the wallet and papers, finally looked up. The prisoner returned his glance calmly. The official looked away.

'From now on,' he barked, 'you are no longer Wurmbrand. Your name is Vasile Georgescu. Remember that! Vasile Georgescu.'

He made a motion of dismissal.

A little later, from the plank bed that provided his only seating accommodation, Richard Wurmbrand examined the tiny, bare, concrete cell in which he was confined. The only illumination came from a small, barred window so high up in the wall that he could not reach it to see out. If the thin sunshine still brought a promise of spring to Bucharest on its wide plain between the mountains and the sea, he would have no means of telling, for the grimy panes acted more as a blind than a window.

Wryly, he contemplated the new name he had been given: Vasile Georgescu. It was as if, in England, he had been called 'John Smith'. The Communists were determined that he should lose his identity under a common name. Even his guards were not to know how famous was the man they were watching, in case they were questioned outside. Pastor Richard Wurmbrand, like so many other Christians and Jews and intellectuals in Communist-occupied Rumania, was to disappear without trace.

CHAPTER I

The Carpenter's Reward

RUMANIA IS ONE of the group of countries that are known collectively as 'The Balkans'. To a generation that grew up between the two World Wars, its name is synonymous with musical comedy and the Orient Express. To the younger generation, more acquainted with rock musicals than musical comedy, with jet travel rather than railways, Rumania is unfamiliar territory. It is not a part of Europe much studied in the geography syllabus of western schools, except as being rich in oil and having the Danube delta on its coast, yet those two factors have been the cause of much of Rumania's troubled history. The Danube has provided access for invaders and, in today's world, oil means power.

The hundred and fifty miles of coastline where the Danube empties itself into the Black Sea through a myriad of sluggish, meandering channels, makes up less than one twelfth of Rumania's long frontier. To the north and east lies the U.S.S.R., to the west, Hungary and Yugoslavia. To the south, separated from Rumania along most of the border by the waters of the River Danube, lies Bulgaria.

The country has seen a constant movement of settlers and invaders along the Danube waterway. Dacians discovered the country's rich valleys and fertile plains a thousand years before Christ. Greek traders built cities along the Black Sea coast. The Emperor Trajan made the country a province of the Roman Empire. Goths and Huns and Tartars invaded it. Germans settled in it. Hungary annexed part of it. Turkey swallowed the country whole into its vast Ottoman Empire and kept it suppressed for four hundred years. Little wonder, then, that it became a country with a mixed population containing a number of minority groups: Hungarians, Germans, gypsies, Jews and many others.

Richard Wurmbrand belonged to two of these groups. He himself is a native-born Rumanian but his family, as the name suggests, was of German extraction from the German-speaking province of Bukovina. Indeed, the family always spoke German at home. Moreover, they were Jewish. Into this family Richard was born in Bucharest on 24th March, 1909.

He grew up in a country at war. When the Congress of Berlin gave Rumania its independence in 1878, it also gave the country a German princeling as its king. He was still on the throne when World War I broke out so Rumania, naturally, was on the side of Germany. However, in 1916 old King Carol died and his successor, Ferdinand, whose wife (Queen Marie) was a granddaughter of Queen Victoria, switched the country's allegiance to the Allies. Immediately, an army of Germans, Bulgarians and Turks invaded Rumania and occupied three-quarters of the country, including the capital itself.

It was a dreadful time of starvation and epidemics. To crown the suffering of the Wurmbrand family, Richard's father died in the 1918 epidemic of Spanish flu. His mother was left to provide food and clothing for Richard and his three older brothers. There was never enough to eat; only second-hand clothes to wear — but there were books in the house, many books, for Richard's father, a dentist, had been a man of taste and culture. Although Richard's education in war-torn Bucharest was scanty, such was his love of reading that by the time he was ten he had read every book he could find, even the sceptical writings of Voltaire. Young and impressionable, with no father to discuss and argue the ideas he was absorbing, by the time he was fourteen he was a convinced atheist. He was not just indifferent to religion; he considered it positively harmful to the human mind. As he read more and more atheistic, revolutionary books, he grew into a young man with revolutionary ideas, ready to suffer and to fight for these pro-Communist ideas and ideals.

Yet when God has a great work to be done, He can use the most unlikely tools. Saul of Tarsus was among those who stoned Stephen, the first Christian martyr, yet as St. Paul men revere him as one of the first and greatest missionaries, a man whose writings have helped to turn the world upside down. Matthew was a hated tax-collector yet he became a disciple of Jesus and in the first Gospel he has left a tender and moving record of Our Lord's brief ministry. So it was not mere chance that the young atheist, Wurmbrand, found himself continually being drawn into synagogues and churches, always seeking a God he was convinced did not exist — but he found little there that was an inspiration for him.

The synagogue services were all in Hebrew which he did not understand and the rabbis seemed always too busy to notice the young enquirer in their congregation. There was equally little comfort to be found in the Christian churches he visited. The ritual was complicated, the sermons dull, and the Roman Catholic Church at that time conducted its services in Latin which he could not follow. Yet churches held a strange and inexplicable fascination for him.

Perhaps this stemmed from an incident which occurred when he was eight years old and which he has never forgotten. His father had, briefly, moved his family and practice to Istanbul in the vain hope that conditions might be better there than in Rumania. On the way home from school with a small Christian friend, Richard and the other boy stopped at the Catholic Church.

'Hang on a minute,' said the friend. 'I have to give a message to the priest from my father.'

He disappeared. It was the first time little Richard had ever been inside a church. It seemed very strange. There was a sweet and unfamiliar smell that he would later come to know as incense. The holy pictures on the walls and the Stations of the Cross were interesting but no more, for the child had never heard the name 'Christ' in his life. He wondered who the old man with the beard was who came out through a side door with his friend. Presently, the old man came over to Richard and patted him on the head.

'Well, little fellow, and what can I do for you?' he asked.

'Nothing,' stammered Richard, overcome.

The old priest smiled. 'But I am a disciple of One who has told me always to do good to other people, so I must do something for you.'

Timidly, Richard ventured that he would like a drink of water and the priest brought it to him. He never forgot the incident and perhaps, subconsciously, hoped as the years went by that the Catholic Church would some day again fulfil his now greater needs. He would enter a church and see people kneeling before a statue of the Virgin Mary, saying their prayer 'Hail, Mary, full of grace'. He would think to himself, 'Perhaps if I kneel by them and listen and say the same words, something will happen.' But nothing did happen for Wurmbrand; the image of the Virgin remained stone.

He found even less to attract him in the Greek Orthodox Church to which eighty per cent of the population of Rumania belonged. He could not reconcile their expressed hatred of his own kind with their professed Christianity. Was not the Jesus they worshipped a Jew? Was not His Mother a Jewess? Yet a Greek Orthodox priest set his dogs on Wurmbrand because he, too, was a Jew.

It was said of Rumania that 'Foreigners and Jews run the country because the Rumanians are too lazy to run it for themselves'. In the thirties, the country was rich and prosperous and a man with little scruple could soon make his fortune. Richard Wurmbrand entered the race for material success. Ambitious, intelligent and with a formidable energy,

he soon outstripped his more complacent Gentile com-
patriots and by the time he was twenty-five, he was already
comfortably off as a stockholder. Honesty was not neces-
sarily for him the best policy so he found it easy to dismiss
'sharp practice' as 'clever dealing'.

He was a handsome young man, tall and broad-shoul-
dered, with a high forehead and deep-set, very blue eyes. He
was never short of a girl friend to escort round the night-
clubs and cabarets of Bucharest. The capital had earned its
title 'Paris of the Balkans' as much for its gay night-life as for
its elegant boulevards and parks. In the sensuous and dec-
adent atmosphere of pre-war Bucharest, Richard set out to
gratify his every appetite. Drink, dancing, food, sex — he
tried them all but still felt a nagging discontent. Nothing
tasted as delightful as it promised to do.

One summer evening, he was leaning over the balcony of
his home feeling sour and angry. His mother had been urging
him to marry and settle down. She had found him a suitable
match in a young Jewish girl of substance, an heiress with a
dowry of a million *lei* and an interest in her family's business.
He was tempted by the dowry and the inheritance but the
girl herself held no attraction for him. As he leaned over the
balcony, he saw his uncle approaching, accompanied by a
pretty, dark, petite girl he had not met before.

'If I could have a girl like *her*,' he thought, 'I wouldn't
care about the million *lei*.'

The girl was Sabina Oster, a young Rumanian from Czernowitz. She was on vacation from her chemistry studies in
Paris and she did not return to Paris after that first meeting
with Richard; instead, she found employment in Bucharest.
The young couple went out together every evening. They
had much in common: they were both Jews who had put
aside their religion, they both loved the gay night-life of the
capital. They were madly in love and married on October
23rd, 1935. As a concession to their respective parents, particularly to Sabina's who were strictly Orthodox Jews, they

were married in the synagogue with all the traditional religious ceremony. As is customary at Jewish weddings, a wineglass was smashed on the floor to remind them of Jerusalem trodden under the feet of the Gentiles but this meant nothing either to Richard or Sabina. Although the rabbi who married them knew that Richard was a convinced, even militant atheist, he made no attempt on this most solemn occasion to talk to the young people about God.

Not that it would have had much effect at the time. Richard and Sabina were a completely worldly couple, flinging themselves frenetically into a round of gay parties and dances. They had no desire for a family; a baby would interfere with their pleasure.

The bubble burst after less than a year of marriage. Richard began to be troubled by a persistent cough so went to see his doctor. He returned to Sabina with the news that he had tuberculosis, perhaps originating in the privations of his childhood years but certainly triggered off by the rackety life he was now leading. Even in the 'thirties, tuberculosis was a dreaded disease and for some time it seemed likely that Richard would die. He was very frightened. There was no logical reason why he should be so for his atheistic reasoning told him that there was nothing after death, that his body would just revert to the minerals of which it was compounded. Yet every instinct warned him that there *must* be something more. After all, what was the point of anything in this life if there were nothing to follow — *but what would it be?* Would there *really* be a Judgment to face? The fear of what might lie ahead terrified him.

He was sent to a sanatorium high up in the Carpathians. It was a beautiful place, with great views across the valleys to forest-clad mountains beyond, but even in such lovely surroundings, Richard could not find rest. He was an atheist, but atheism did not give him peace in his heart. In his despair and anxiety, he found himself struggling to pray. It was a strange prayer.

'God,' he challenged the unknown. 'I know you do not exist. But if perchance you *do* exist (which I deny), it is for you to reveal yourself to me. It is not my duty to seek you.'

As he prayed this reluctant prayer, Richard began to think about the past, about the girls he had seduced, the mother he had grieved, the wife he now seemed to have failed. Tears came easily in his weak state but they brought some relief, and when Sabina came to see him on one of her fortnightly visits, she found him quieter, less resentful of his illness.

He told her about a book he had been reading to while away the long hours in bed. It was about the Brothers Ratisbonne who had founded an Order with the purpose of converting Jews to Christ. It seemed incredible to Richard that anyone should think the matter important enough to bother. Then it was borne in upon him with something of a shock that *he* himself must be one of the Jews the Order was praying for, even though they did not know him by name. It was a humbling thought. If strangers could consider his life so important, had he been right or fair to throw it away by riotous living? He tried to explain this to Sabina but she was impatient with his arguments.

'What are you worrying about?' she demanded. 'There's nothing wrong in what we do. We are young. Youth is to be enjoyed.'

But Richard was beginning to question the manner of the enjoyment.

After some months in the sanatorium, the doctors felt he was sufficiently recovered to leave. It was the spring of 1937 and Richard decided to go to a village in the mountains to convalesce. Rumania has twelve thousand villages and he could have chosen any one of them, but God directed him to Noua. Unbeknown to Richard, the carpenter of that particular village, an old man called Christian Wolfkes, had for some years been praying like this:

'Dear God, I have one very great wish which I beseech

you to grant me. I long to bring a Jew to Christ before I die, for Jesus himself was from the Jewish people. But I am poor and old and sick. I cannot go out looking for a Jew myself and there are no Jews in our village. Please, God, bring a Jew here to our village and I will do my best to bring him to Christ.'

In Richard Wurmbrand, the old man saw the answer to his prayer.

He gave him a Bible to read. The printed word, irrespective of its content, had always fascinated Richard so he read the carpenter's Bible. As a Jew, however non-practising, he was already in some measure acquainted with the Old Testament so he left that aside. But the New Testament was virgin territory for him. Day after day, he lay on the sofa in the cottage reading about Jesus. He was fascinated by the man, by his direct approach, his undeviating honesty, his devastating logic in argument. He was impressed that this man, Jesus, could show love even to sinners. He read on, stirred more than he cared to admit by the story of Jesus's selfless life of service. But to what end? Christ had been crucified and he offered no easier fate to those who sought to follow his principles.

'You'll never have me for a disciple,' Richard said stubbornly. 'I want money, travel, pleasure. This illness is suffering enough. Yours is the way of the cross, and even if it is the way of truth as well, *I won't follow it.*'

Richard hesitates to tell what followed in case he should be thought to be exaggerating. He saw no vision of Christ but, he says, he was vividly aware of his presence and it seemed as if a voice spoke clearly to him: 'Do not fear the cross! You will find it the greatest of joys.'

When he went back to his reading of the New Testament, every passage his eye alighted on seemed to be telling him how sinful was his own life. Christ's outlook was so pure; Richard's so tainted. His nature was so selfless; Richard's had been greedy for experience. All Richard's certainties began to crumble. He found he *needed* the friendship of this man Jesus if he was to salvage anything from the wreck of his life. This *man*? Surely he must be God after all; there could be no other explanation of the wisdom and truth of what he read.

'I was like the man in the ancient Chinese story,' Richard was to write many years later, 'trudging exhausted under the sun, who came on a great oak and rested in its shade. "What a happy chance I found you!" he said. But the oak replied, "It is no chance. I have been waiting for you for 400 years." Christ had waited all my life for me. Now we met.'

Richard's conversion to Christianity was a terrible blow to his wife. Though she had latterly shown scant observance of the Jewish religion, she was steeped from childhood in the history of the persecution of her people by Christians. Like the children of other Orthodox Jewish families, she had been forbidden to mention Christ's name in speech. When she passed a church as a child, she was ordered to turn away her head. She could still remember having her hair pulled by bigger girls at school because she was 'a dirty little Jewess'. The Nazis in Germany were set on a course of persecution of Jews; and already in Rumania the Fascist organisation of Greenshirts, Christian in name if not in fact, had begun their ghastly pogroms. Jewish students were thrown out of the windows at the University. Other Jews were impaled on meat hooks in the market and labelled 'Kosher Meat'. Now her husband was to join the enemies and persecutors of her race. When she heard that Richard was to be baptised into the Christian faith, she contemplated suicide.

Richard was patient with her. He talked to her of Christ. He took her, frightened but also a little curious, to see the inside of a church. He showed her the pictures of Jesus and His mother and pointed out that they were Jews. He opened the Prayer Book and showed her that the Commandments printed there for Christians to obey were the same that she had learned from the Book of Moses. He showed her the

Psalms and she realised that they were the same Psalms of David that she had heard read in the synagogue as a child. Richard showed her the Old Testament prophecies that foretold Christ's coming. Surely she could see that Christianity was simply the Jewish faith opened to all the nations of the earth. Still she was not convinced; and anyway, she did not want to spend Sundays in church. She hated the idea of giving up the gay life she enjoyed so much.

Richard tried another approach.

'All right,' he conceded one Sunday evening when she protested at his attending service. 'If you want to see a film, we'll both see a film — because I love you.'

They went into the city centre and Richard went from theatre to theatre, studying the posters and stills outside. 'We'll go to this one,' he decided at last. Sabina was surprised; it was a very suggestive film. Two hours later when they emerged from the cinema she was even more surprised to hear him say: 'You go off home now. I think I'll stay up in town and pick up a girl.'

'*What did you say!*' Sabina was outraged.

'But you wanted me to come to the theatre tonight,' Richard replied quietly. 'You saw what happened in the film. Why should I not do the same? Every man becomes what he looks at, and if you want me to watch films like that night after night, can you blame me if I turn into a bad husband? On the other hand, if you want me to be a good husband, let me go to church — and come with me sometimes.'

Sabina had to concede that he was right about the film — but she still hankered after the gay parties Richard wanted to put behind them. One evening, to her delight, he did agree to accept an invitation. When they arrived at the friend's apartment, many of the guests were already very drunk. The air was thick with cigarette smoke. One or two couples were petting in corners. Even to Sabina, the party seemed pretty awful. 'Let's go home,' she whispered after a very short time. 'If we slip away now, no-one will notice.'

'Why leave?' protested Richard. 'We've only just come.'

So they stayed on at the party where the drinking became more rowdy, the petting more open. Sabina hated it. 'Can't we leave now,' she begged Richard again at midnight.

'It's far too early,' he replied airily. 'The night is young yet.'

Time and again she implored him to leave and time and again he refused. Only when he saw that she was utterly sickened by the whole sordid occasion did he agree to take her home. They came out of the smoke-laden atmosphere into the cold clean air of early morning.

'Richard!' Sabina exclaimed. 'I'm going straight to your pastor's house to ask him to baptise me as a Christian. It will be like taking a bath after all that filth.'

Richard laughed. 'You've waited so long,' he said. 'Surely you can now wait until the morning. Let the poor pastor have his sleep.'

CHAPTER 2

The Gathering Storm

IN ORDER TO appreciate the problems that the Wurmbrands had now to face as Christian Jews, it is necessary to understand the political situation of the time.

Europe, between the two World Wars, saw the spread of Totalitarianism — that is, rule by one party only with no opposition. This totalitarianism took two different and violently opposed forms.

At the extreme 'Left' was Communism, based on the writings of Karl Marx. This advocated the overthrow of all existing forms of government. It allowed no private enterprise, no personal freedom. Communism in its present form spread from Russia across national barriers. It kept, and still keeps, a ruthless hold on its subjects in every way, including their minds. Skilful propaganda controls their thinking, secret police their actions. Religion, with its emphasis on individual responsibility, is denounced as superstition. The State has replaced God.

Totalitarianism of the extreme 'Right' was called Fascism. This came into being in the chaos following the violent upheaval of World War I. European countries became impoverished by the war, traditions of centuries were upset, life was insecure. In such conditions, Communism began to spread rapidly. The middle classes, however, were apprehensive of its onward march. They were afraid of losing their national identity and were bewildered by the loss of their money as their country's finances collapsed, so they looked for strong leaders. Thus the stage was set for the rise of Mussolini in Italy, of Hitler in Germany, of Codreanu in

Rumania, and many others. All introduced 'Fascist' régimes under different names, all offering a strong one-party government, intensely nationalistic in feeling. Great stress was laid on keeping the nation 'pure' and to this end attacks were made on minority groups — in particular, in Germany and Rumania, on Jews who were blamed for all these countries' financial troubles. The attacks served also to divert attention from the loss of individual freedom under a dictatorship.

In Rumania, Corneliu Zelea Codreanu, claiming to have been inspired by the Archangel, founded his 'Legion of St. Michael', with the declared aim of cleansing the country of all Jews. This organisation developed into the Iron Guard, often known as 'Greenshirts' from the colour of the military-style uniform they wore. These were the men who had so cruelly attacked Jews in the pogroms.

It was some time, however, before Richard and Sabina came into conflict with either Communism or Fascism. The hostility they met at the beginning of their Christian life came from their own people, the Jews.

When Christ spoke to him in the carpenter's house and said 'Do not fear the cross; you will find it the greatest of joys', Richard little realised how soon he would be expected to take up that cross in following his Lord. He and Sabina had no desire to quarrel with anyone; all they wanted was rest from the life that had gone before, particularly after a little son, Mihai, was born to them in January 1939.

Richard was to write some years later: 'A calm life ... raises new storms; one's religion is attacked, one must defend it, and so, without having wished it, one is at war again. We have actively to put into practice faith and love, and only God knows why, as sons of peace, we do not bring peace, but a sword.'

It was dreadful for the Wurmbrands to be called 'traitors' by their former Jewish friends because they had become Christian; but the hostility they now met among their own kind was only a challenge to a man of Richard's temperament.

Burning with zeal to show the truth of Christ, Richard sought out the rabbi who had conducted his wedding service. He was met with bland indifference. Other rabbis he argued with reproached him for abandoning 'the faith of his fathers'. Richard could not persuade them that faith was something you could not inherit from your fathers but was a matter of personal conviction; each man must have his own living experience of God. The rabbis he met were too firmly entrenched in their rigid thinking to be open to persuasion so Richard turned his attention to Jews who were not rabbis.

With a clarity that was not blinded by centuries of anti-Semitic prejudice, Richard could recognise how immense is the potential of the Jewish race. It was no accident of history that God chose them as His people, that He sent His son into the world as a Jew. Even without accepting Christ, the Jews have been a brilliant race, producing men of the highest intellectual calibre — great scientists like Einstein, great painters like Chagall, composers, musicians, writers. If only the intellectual passion, the brilliant intelligence of the Jewish people could be harnessed for *Christ*, with what an unequalled beauty could the Church be invested! It could be on fire with love for mankind; it could transform the world! Now, at the beginning of his own Christian life, Richard felt that God had called him to bring Jews to Christ. He did not know how he would carry out the work but he had faith that the way would be shown to him.

It was not easy, however, for the new convert to find the Church that was founded by Jesus. Various Christian denominations in Rumania at that time seemed still to be rooted in mediaeval ideas about Jews and were as anti-Semitic (that is, 'Jew-hating') as the Fascist administration they supported. Richard found the Christian scene a tragic one. Was this in the spirit of Jesus who said 'I was sent to the lost sheep of the house of Israel'? Men had made of Christianity such a complicated thing, full of sectarian differences and formal ritual. Surely there was need for the simplicity of the early Church? The message of the Gospels seemed so clear to him: God is love. If Christianity could truly be demonstrated to be love — of God, of one's neighbour, of one's enemies — then even the Jews must become converted to it, for they were thirsty for love in a world that persecuted their race so cruelly.

Richard found a job as Secretary to the Anglican Mission to Jews in Bucharest. This was a missionary church and centre set up by the Church of England for the purpose of converting some of Rumania's thousands of Jews to Christianity. Rev. George Stevens was the pastor.

In his enthusiasm to do his best for the Mission, it was not easy for Richard always to avoid his old ways. When an insurance company brought a claim against the Mission, it seemed quite easy for Richard to slip into his former ways and offer a bribe to the Insurance Agent to drop the claim. He boasted of this to the Mission head.

'But are we really liable?' asked Mr. Stevens.

'Of course,' Richard replied.

'Then you were wrong to offer the bribe; we should pay what we owe.'

It took Richard some little time to accept that there could be no double standards for a Christian. But he was happy at the Mission, delighted that a door had opened for him on to the work he felt called to do.

The very first soul he won for the Lord was Clarutza, a Jewish girl of sixteen. Although she would consider herself a convert of Richard's, it was in fact she who completed *his* conversion. Just as he was finding it difficult to renounce completely some of his former business methods, equally he still could not easily shake off the desire to make a lot of money without any effort. Although his conscience told him that buying lottery tickets was not in the Christian tradition, none the less he bought one, for the prize was a very large sum of money. Did Clarutza guess?

'Brother,' she asked him. 'Have you taken a ticket in the lottery?'

'Of course not,' Richard lied readily, though the ticket was in his pocket as he spoke.

It is easy to tell a lie; less easy to live with one. The knowledge of his deception kept nagging at his conscience until he could bear it no longer and he had to confess. He told the story at the Mission on the following Sunday, in front of the whole congregation. There was a brief pause then, one after another, Christian Jews stood up and openly confessed to falsehoods, frauds and thefts they had kept hidden in their hearts. It was an occasion of great blessing for all who were present.

Richard was not yet ordained a pastor but he did his best to be a missionary in his own country. He felt he just had to tell everybody he met about the wonderful Good News of Jesus. He would buttonhole Jewish people on trains, in the street and on park benches to talk to them about Christ. He also distributed leaflets and literature about the Christian faith. Strangely enough, there was a need for such literature to be distributed even among Christians, for the Orthodox Church did not allow its members to read the Gospels for themselves.

One Sunday morning in the summer of 1939, Richard and Clarutza went to Sinaia, the beautiful mountain resort some sixty miles north of Bucharest where the King had his summer residence. They set up their stall of Gospels and pamphlets outside the church.

Richard's face was unmistakably Jewish; so was Clarutza's. In those uneasy days, all things evil were attributed to the Jewish race. A suspicious policeman, convinced that the two Jews in charge of the stall could be up to no good, approached Richard and asked him his name.

'Wurmbrand,' replied Richard, which took the policeman

aback. It was a German name, not Jewish. None the less, the policeman persisted and asked to see their identity cards. These, of course, revealed that Richard and Clarutza were indeed of Jewish origin. 'JEW' was stamped across every Jewish identity card, even if its holder was a Christian. The policeman was outraged. How did they, as Jews, *dare* to sell Christian literature? They were desecrating something holy! He promptly arrested them and marched them off to the police station. But it was Sunday morning and most of the police were off duty. The prisoners were left in charge of a young constable to await the arrival of the police inspector who would determine what action to take about their heinous crime!

Suddenly the telephone rang, asking for immediate help at the scene of an accident. The constable hurried off, leaving the 'prisoners' alone in the police station. Richard and Clarutza waited; the whole situation was so farcical, they were intrigued to see how it would end. At last the Police Inspector arrived, unaware that the man and girl in the waiting room were the 'criminals' he was to interrogate.

'Good morning, Inspector,' said Richard, seizing the initiative. 'My name is Wurmbrand. This young lady and I want to sell religious literature in your town. Do we need your permission?'

It did not occur to the Inspector to check whether or not they were Jewish nor, indeed, whether they had already sold their literature.

'Have you a permit from the Ministry of Culture?' he asked.

'Oh dear, no. Should we have had one?' Richard was all innocence.

'Then I'm afraid I can't give you permission to sell your literature here.'

'Ah well,' sighed Richard. 'It looks as if we shall have to go home again. Good morning, Inspector!'

'Good morning.'

Without waiting for any more questions to be asked, Richard and Clarutza hurried from the police station, stopped the first taxi they saw and left the town. Richard's quick wit and sharp intelligence when faced with a crisis were often to stand him in good stead when in later years he had to face prison interrogation.

In September of 1939, war broke out between Germany on one side and Britain and France on the other. King Carol II was nominally on the side of the Allies who had guaranteed Rumania's neutrality. However, Germany was a nearer neighbour and in March of that year he had considered it prudent to make an economic treaty whereby Rumania's vast resources, especially her oil, were placed at the disposal of Germany. The king's policy of keeping a foot in both camps was eventually to lead to his own downfall and that of his country.

Throughout the spring and summer of 1940, Rumania vacillated between allegiance to Germany or to the Allies. Russia was threatening Rumania's northern border, claiming the province of Bessarabia. As the Allied fortunes in Europe ebbed, Rumania began to look more and more towards Germany for support against Russia.

It was a fearful time for the Jews. They were terrified of a take-over by Russia for the Communists had always been anti-Semitic in their policy. Equally, they feared the influence of Hitler's Germany — a country bent on the extermination of their race. At home, the Iron Guard openly flaunted their power.

The Guard had been temporarily disbanded in 1938 when their founder, Codreanu, had been arrested and executed. Many of his organisation had fled to Germany where they drilled and trained, becoming more Nazi even than the Nazis themselves. Now, in the summer of 1940, following an amnesty from the king, the Iron Guard re-emerged under a new leader, Horia Sima. The exiles returned from Germany — lean, fit and hard, and dedicated in their hatred.

They swaggered openly through the streets, while Jews throughout Rumania trembled. Those who could afford it, fled the country. Those who were poor remained and suffered, or committed suicide. Goods and houses were seized, investments appropriated. It is difficult for people in democratic countries such as Britain or America to appreciate the scope of the terror unleashed by the Fascists on the Jews.

By August 1940 it appeared to the Rumanian Government that the Allies were defeated. The British Army had retreated through Dunkirk; Paris had fallen; Norway, Denmark and the Low Countries were all overrun. It was time to ally the country openly with Germany.

Naturally, such English people as remained in Bucharest felt it advisable to leave, including the head of the Anglican Mission where Richard worked. Since there was no minister to carry on the work of the church, Richard offered to take on the work himself. He studied and was in due course ordained as a pastor.

From now on, he was in constant danger. He was an obvious target for the Iron Guard. In his home and in his church, Richard offered Jews sanctuary from persecution. It did not matter that he himself was a Christian Jew and that his mission was to convert other Jews to Christianity. He was of Jewish *blood* and that sufficed. Jews were anathema not only to the Iron Guard but also, to its shame, to the Orthodox Church. At that time, the Church supported the Fascists in their campaign of terror. Murder walked the streets of Bucharest and of every other big city.

One Sunday from his pulpit Richard saw a group of Iron Guard in their recognisable green shirts file into the back of his church. He could see that they were armed, although the congregation, facing towards the pulpit, were unaware of their presence. Richard determined that if this were to be his last sermon, it should be a good one. He was speaking about the hands of Jesus, how they had healed the sick and cradled children; how they had stretched out in blessing; how they had touched lepers and had been nailed to the Cross.

'But *you*!' he suddenly thundered. 'What have *you* done with *your* hands?'

The congregation looked at him in amazement; their hands held only their prayer-books!

'Do you call yourselves Christians?' continued Richard in passionate accusation. 'You, who kill and beat and torture innocent people? Cleanse your hands, you sinners!'

For some reason, the Greenshirts did not break up the service. Though they glowered with rage and stood with their guns drawn, they allowed Richard to finish his sermon, and say the prayer and benediction. The congregation filed out — hastily as they saw the reason for Richard's outburst. As the last person left, Richard stepped down from the pulpit and moved quickly behind a curtain. He could hear running footsteps and shouts of 'Where's Wurmbrand? After him!'

But he was prepared for just such an eventuality. Behind the curtain was a secret door leading through a series of corridors out into a side street. Once through the door and with it safely locked behind him, Richard fled.

CHAPTER 3

Fascist Terror

SOMETIMES IN THE midst of gaiety on a day of warm sunshine, one will suddenly shiver. It is almost as if some Spirit of Times to Come moves past and one feels the cold draught of his trailing garments. Some premonition of this sort had happened to Richard in the early days of his courtship. One evening, he had said a strange and unexpected thing to Sabina: 'You will suffer a lot if you marry me.' The reality of that suffering, the reality of Jesus's words 'If any man will come after me, let him ... take up his cross' began now to reveal itself to the young couple. They were in constant danger.

One day a member of the Iron Guard was found dead in a street of Bucharest. No-one knew what had happened but members of the Jewish community knew only too well that they would be blamed and that reprisals would be taken against them. A day or so later, Richard was sitting at home when two young men of Jewish appearance asked to see him. They said they had something on their conscience they wished to confess.

'Go ahead,' said Richard.

They told him that they had been responsible for the murder. Richard was dismayed.

'How could you commit a crime like that?'

'He was a Fascist,' they said. 'He deserved to die.'

This reply made Richard angry. 'Then why have you come to me?' he demanded. 'I can understand your asking my advice if you were ashamed of the crime you have committed, but you seem to glory in it. What you have done *is* a crime. Even if a man is a Fascist, he should still be treated as a human being. Did you not think that he could have a mother or a wife? If he is our enemy, we must repay his hatred with love. We must not kill him.'

And he sent the young men on their way.

That was not the end of the story. Some months later, when the Iron Guard had been overthrown, one of the same two young men came again to see Richard.

'I must tell you how you escaped certain death,' he said.

He went on to describe how he was in fact a Communist who had been arrested by the Iron Guard while distributing propaganda leaflets. He was tortured and, in order to escape further ordeal, agreed to act as an *agent provocateur* for the Iron Guard. The idea was that he and the other young man (who was a member of the Iron Guard) would pretend to be Jews. They would visit any place where they might find Jews gathered together and would start pro-Communist discussions, at the same time criticising and insulting the Fascists. Anyone who agreed with their opinions would later be arrested by the Iron Guard and beaten up. With this plan in mind, knowing that Richard was the leader of a Christian Mission to Jews, they had called at his home and confessed to a murder they had not committed.

'We never thought we should hear a Jew say that Greenshirts should be loved!' the young man said.

Richard's truly Christian approach had saved his life.

The Government permit for the Anglican Mission had become invalid when the Iron Guard came to power; it was necessary to apply for a new one. But how could Richard, a Jew, dare even to enter a Government Office to apply for such a permit when the declared policy of the Government was anti-Semitic? There was still one Englishman remaining in Bucharest who worked at the Mission, a young man called Roger Allison. He and Richard decided to visit an Inspector of the Ministry of Cults in his home. This Inspector was in fact an Orthodox priest who was also a member of the Iron

Guard. When Richard introduced himself, the priest was most affable. Wurmbrand is a German name, and Germans at that time were treated with deference in Rumania. Imagine the Inspector's surprise when Richard disclosed that he was a Christian Jew seeking a permit for his Christian Mission to Jews!

'We don't want any exceptions to be made in our case,' said Richard. 'We don't expect to be treated differently from other Jews just because we are Christian. All we ask is the right to worship.'

The Inspector/priest burst out laughing. It seemed to him a great joke that a Jew should have been baptised. 'Of course, it is only your *skin* that is baptised,' he said. 'You could not possibly become a *real* Christian.'

'How right you are,' agreed Richard. 'It is difficult enough for anyone to be truly Christlike and it is doubly difficult for us Jews who are so new to the task. But we *are* trying in our community. We do beg you to give us a chance to try to improve.'

The Inspector continued for a long time to mock and insult Richard and the Mission but Richard continued to answer humbly, admitted that he and his fellows fell far short of the ideal standard of Christians but insisted that they sincerely believed and, if only given the opportunity to worship, would seek to do better. Suddenly the priest changed his tone. 'I have been deliberately testing you,' he said, 'and I have discovered that you are worthier of bearing the name of Christian than I am. You shall have your permit.'

The Wurmbrands' was not a luxurious home. Indeed, it was only an apartment on the northern outskirts of Bucharest where the rents were low. The other apartments in the block were occupied by members of the anti-Semitic Orthodox Church so the Wurmbrands were viewed with suspicion, though tolerated because they were Christian. Round the courtyard were pasted big posters of Codreanu,

the founder of the Legion of St. Michael. He had been a
thug and a Jew-baiter but now he was being almost can-
onised. The apartment block was not a friendly place for
Richard and Sabina to live.

That was at the beginning.

But Richard always had a wonderful gift for finding the
right word for the person he was seeking to win. He was once
described, derogatorily, as 'a great actor' but he took this as a
compliment. 'I cannot see how it is possible to be a good
missionary,' he said, 'unless one has a certain artistic flair,
and a knack of playing different rôles.'

Using this gift, Richard set to work to win over his hostile
neighbours. One man snarled at him: 'You Jews have never
done a damned thing that's any good.' Richard was standing
by the parlour door at the time, watching the man's wife
sewing. He replied, 'That's a fine sewing-machine. What
make is it? A Singer! Hold on — wasn't that invented by a
Jew? Really, you know, if you think Jews are so useless,
you'd better get rid of that sewing-machine!' No wonder the
neighbour began to laugh. Gradually Richard wore down
the unfriendliness of the other residents of the block. He
could be charming, he could be direct, he could command or
he could cajole. And, as his wife Sabina has said, 'his blue
eyes could look into your soul'.

So their neighbours did not betray them when their house
was used as a refuge for the homeless and the persecuted.
Every day, Christians and Jews in trouble of some kind,
gypsies, beggars, anyone in need would come to their door.
No-one was ever turned away. Mihai has written how even if
Sabina had to 'slice the bread a little thinner, or stretch the
soup with water', none the less there was always a place at
the table for the hungry stranger.

She had become a radiant Christian. Richard was the dynamic crusader against cruelty and oppression. She gave no
less effective Christian witness in her gentle acts of love. A
friend said of her: 'It seemed as if no-one in Rumania got

married or had a baby or encountered trouble but they came
to Sabina for advice.'

In September of 1940, King Carol was forced to abdicate.
For a brief period, the ordinary people of Rumania hoped
that sanity would be restored to their country. Carol had
been an autocrat; and in endeavouring to placate both Germany and the Allies, he had succeeded in pleasing nobody
and had lost his country's trust. Now King Carol's son,
Michael, succeeded to the throne. The country had hopes of
a 'New Age' under the new young ruler but he was very
young and the real power lay with the Prime Minister, Ion
Antonescu, who had to continue to use the Iron Guard to
keep control. Conscription was introduced. Meat and petrol
were rationed. More than seventy per cent of Rumania's
output had to go to Germany. The Rumanian cow was being
well and truly milked. Far from witnessing the dawn of a new
age, Rumanians were seeing the sunset of freedom.

After a time, the Prime Minister tried to dispense with the
services of the Iron Guard but that was easier wished than
done. A vicious power struggle developed. There was
fighting in the streets of Bucharest between rival factions,
bloody massacres as Fascists and their opponents killed each
other off. At this time, Richard and Sabina even helped the
families of Iron Guard who were suffering in Antonescu's
purge. One family, in great distress, were about to commit
suicide when Richard came to their rescue. He was criti-
cised for extending his help to anti-Semites but he insisted
that it was Christ's command that we should love our
enemies.

'We must not be selective in our good deeds,' Richard has
written. 'The enemy we have conquered must also have our
help. But any help given to an enemy when he is *in power* is
wrong, because it makes us his accomplices.'

Eventually, Antonescu broke the power of the Iron Guard
by calling on Hitler for assistance, but it was at the cost of
the last pretence of neutrality. Rumania now entered the

war actively on the side of Germany and the country itself was occupied by German troops.

The hounding of Jews increased in intensity and persecution bit deep into the Wurmbrand household.

All Sabina's family were deported from their home near the frontier town of Czernowitz — her parents, her brother and three sisters, along with many relatives and friends. It was winter; many of the people collapsed in the snow; others starved to death; numbers were shot. Sabina never heard from any of her family again.

She and Richard risked punishment by giving sanctuary in their home to Jews hunted by the Nazis. More than this, Richard spoke out fearlessly against the system that could encourage such terror. He preached with power and people listened. He would stand up in any church that would invite him to preach, no matter what its denomination, speaking of the love of Christ, bringing courage and hope to frightened people. He preached in bars, in brothels, in prisons; and when the Nazis and their puppets forbade him to speak, he arranged secret meetings in people's homes and continued his defiant teaching there. He became a rallying point for resistance to the régime. Many times attempts were made to arrest him during meetings but always warning was received in time and the group was able to disperse quickly and unnoticed.

On June 28th, 1941, eleven thousand Jews were butchered in one day in the town of Jassy in north-east Rumania. Seven young Christian Jewish girls managed to survive, along with a Norwegian missionary, Sister Olga. When Richard learned of this he determined to rescue these girls before another massacre overtook them. But how? Jews were forbidden to travel, yet if the girls remained in Jassy their death was certain. Richard devised an ingenious plan. He arranged with a friend in the Police whom he knew to be a sincere Christian to have the girls arrested and brought to Bucharest as prisoners. Richard and Sabina met the train,

took over the prisoners from the Christian policeman who
was escorting them and sheltered them in their home until
their escape to safety could be arranged.

Antonescu's new régime brought further problems for
the Christian Jews of the Mission. Once again, the permit to
worship, extracted so recently and so unexpectedly from the
Iron Guard, became invalid. Moreover, when Rumania
officially entered the war on Germany's side, diplomatic re-
lations were broken off with Britain and the Anglican
Mission to the Jews was dissolved. The Assembly Hall was
closed and the Wurmbrands were evicted from their flat.
The little congregation of about one hundred converted Jews
were now without a home. Fortunately the Rumanian
branch of the Swedish Mission to Israel was prepared to
accommodate Richard and his flock. This was a Lutheran
missionary body similar to the Anglican Mission. However,
Richard would once again have to obtain a permit to hold
meetings.

This time he approached Mr. Sandu, a cabinet minister in
the new government and head of the Ministry of Ecclesi-
astical Affairs. Once again, thanks to his German name,
Richard was granted an interview. He attempted the same
honest approach that had won him his permit on the previous occasion. This time, however, he had no success. The
Minister attempted to refer him to another department
and when Richard said he had already tried them refused his
application altogether.

'The Germans are in our country,' he said. 'We cannot
give permits of this kind to Jews.'

'At that moment,' Richard wrote of this incident, 'God
had taken from me all my powers of reasoning, so that I
completely forgot that I was a Jew, without any rights, in an
anti-Semitic atmosphere, in the office of a minister of state.
All he had to do would be to ring his bell, and I should have
been arrested and should have vanished without a trace.'

When the Minister refused the permit, Richard said to

him: 'All right, Minister. I withdraw my application but we shall continue to meet and to worship at our own risk. But before I leave, I want to remind you of something. The day will come when we shall no longer be ministers of state, clergymen or anything else; we shall all stand naked and trembling before the Throne of God to answer for our deeds. Consider carefully what you may have to answer for when you deny Christians the right to assemble peaceably in order to worship Jesus.'

Richard stopped speaking, dismayed at his own boldness, and waited for the outraged anger, for the arrest he felt must be inevitable. But the Minister did not fly into a rage. Instead, to Richard's amazement, he rose from his chair and asked humbly: 'What can I do to be saved, wretched sinner that I am?'

Richard was touched with awe. It could only be the power of God working through him that had wrought such a change.

So, once again, he had a permit for his Church to assemble. It did not last long. Soon afterwards, Richard and Sabina and several others were arrested on a charge of holding 'illegal religious meetings'. By the time they were released from prison, they found their permit had been cancelled and the cabinet minister who had granted it had been dismissed.

The lack of a permit did not deter them. If the Church could not meet in public, they would worship together in secret, meeting in various homes, each time risking long terms of imprisonment should they be discovered. They developed all manner of ingenious techniques to keep their assemblies from being raided. Only on one occasion were they surprised and even that situation was saved by some quick thinking. The Police had made the mistake of not surrounding the whole block of flats where the meeting was being held. When they knocked on the door, the owner of the apartment took a long time opening up. Then he delayed the police in the entrance. What did they want? Could they identify themselves? And so on. When the police finally made their way into the flat and began their search, they could find no-one there except the members of the family; all the worshippers had escaped through the back windows for the apartment was on the ground floor!

However, Richard's work was so varied and outstanding, his reputation so widespread, it was inevitable that sooner or later the authorities would manage to trap him. If the name 'Wurmbrand' could become synonymous with 'comfort' to Rumania's oppressed, equally it had come to represent 'opposition' to those in authority.

About eleven o'clock one night, Richard was making notes for a sermon when Sabina hurried into the room.

'The police have surrounded the house,' she warned him.

Richard just had time to hide his notes — in themselves enough proof of 'guilt' in the eyes of the police — when those same police pushed their way into the room and declared that he was under arrest. Richard went with them promptly and without protest; he did not want them to search the next room! That was stacked to the ceiling with crates of food which were to be distributed next day among several hundred Protestant Christian women who were interned in the women's prison. The Wurmbrands had taken on the job of distributing such relief on behalf of various oppressed groups whose leaders lacked the courage to do such dangerous work for themselves. Giving aid to prisoners was a serious offence. If the police had found the food, there would have been all manner of awkward questions to face: where had the money come from to buy the food? For whom was it intended? Did they not know it was economic sabotage to hoard food?

Fortunately, Richard was granted his release after only fourteen days' imprisonment on that occasion, thanks to the intervention of the Swedish Ambassador. Although the Ambassador had a responsibility for the Swedish Mission itself, he was really breaking diplomatic rules in interceding for a Rumanian citizen. But the Ambassador had considerable influence in high places. Sweden was a neutral country and through its embassy in Bucharest, Prime Minister Antonescu could keep in touch with Moscow. After all, Germany *might* lose the war! So once again Richard was free to carry on his work.

As the war increased in violence, Richard found other outlets for his passionate Christianity. He provided help for gypsies who, along with Jews and Protestants, were subject to oppression. Where Jewish children had been herded into ghettoes, he organised the rescue of as many as he could and tried to reunite them with parents or relatives. He and his brethren planned escape routes across the border from Hungary for Jews who had managed to escape the Nazi extermination camps. All this was carried out under the noses of the occupying Germans. Richard had a special edition of St. John's Gospel printed and distributed among the German soldiers.

Rumanian troops were fighting alongside the Germans in the attack on Stalingrad and many Russian prisoners-of-war were brought to Rumania. Whenever Richard met any of them, he would take the opportunity to speak to them of Christ. Richard spoke fluent Russian — his father's family came from the province of Bukovina which had changed hands several times between Russia and Rumania — and in meeting Russian soldiers he felt he had a God-given opportunity and a God-given mission.

His very first encounter with a Russian prisoner of war moved him to tears.

'He told me he was an engineer,' Richard wrote afterwards. 'I asked if he believed in God. If he had said "No", I would not have minded it much. It is the right of every man to believe or disbelieve. But when I asked him if he believed in God, he lifted towards me eyes without understanding and said: "I have no such military order to believe. If I have an order I will believe." '

Bucharest was under constant attack from the air by the Russian airforce. As soon as the sirens sounded, Richard would hurry to the nearest air-raid shelter and take the opportunity of preaching the Word of God, thus reaching Rumanians as well as Jews.

The very first air-raid took place on one of the many occasions when Richard was under arrest. He was, in fact, actually in the middle of being tried, along with six other brethren. When the 'Alert' was sounded, the prisoners were bundled into the nearest air-raid shelter by an armed guard and there they were joined by the judge, the lawyers, the court officials and members of the public. The drone of heavy bombers, the whine and crump of falling bombs was terrifying. The shelter shook with the violence of the explosions and dust showered down. Everyone was frightened; somebody screamed. Then, above the moans of terror and the crash of bombs, Richard's voice rang out clearly and calmly: 'Let us all kneel and I will say a prayer.' They all knelt: judge, lawyers, armed guard and public. Richard prayed and everyone crossed themselves and said 'Amen'. Then, without any interruption, Richard went on to preach to an attentive audience about the need always to be prepared to meet one's God.

The 'All Clear' sounded.

Immediately, the guard seized Richard and the other prisoners by the collar and marched them back to the courtroom. The trial was resumed and the judge who, only a short while before, had been on his knees before Richard now sentenced him to a term of imprisonment!

In the years between 1941 and 1944, Richard was gaoled several times by the Fascists and the Nazis before they themselves were overthrown and themselves became the hunted. He endured interrogations and beatings on many occassions but they never broke his spirit. Indeed, these years under Fascist oppression were turned to advantage.

'They taught us,' Richard wrote, 'that physical beatings *could* be endured, that the human spirit with God's help can survive horrible tortures. They taught us the technique of secret Christian work.'

He was to need all this preparation for the far worse ordeal that was soon to come. The tide of war was turning against Germany. Richard was about to face the Communists.

CHAPTER 4

The Pastor

BY THE SPRING of 1944, the Russian army had rolled back
the combined German and Rumanian forces and had
reached the frontier. Rumania had been long enough under
Fascists of one kind or another to recognise that salvation
did not lie that way. An anti-Fascist Communist 'People's
Party' had been formed the previous year, led by Gheorghe
Gheorgiu-Dej. On August 23rd this party toppled the Antonescu régime in a swift, armed coup. King Michael announced his support for the Allies and declared war on
Germany. Now Bucharest was bombed by the Germans instead of the Russians!

Rumania had suffered so much under Fascism that when
the Russian army invaded the country, they were in the beginning welcomed as friends. When the first columns entered
Bucharest on August 31st, 1944, Richard and Sabina went
out on a tram to meet them. This did not mean that they
welcomed Communism to Rumania; rather, they welcomed
the opportunity of reaching with the Good News of Christ
representatives of a people brain-washed into atheism.

There was, of course, an official 'welcome' for the Russians: a rather nervous group of Rumanian Communists
carrying red flags, quavering the Internationale, practising
phrases of welcome in Russian and preparing to hand over
the traditional Rumanian gift of welcome to the
stranger — a loaf of bread, a handful of salt. Richard and
Sabina were not part of the official party. Their presence on
this momentous occasion was the result of one of Richard's
impulsive decisions and they had brought Bibles in Russian

as gifts. But when the first huge Soviet tank came to a halt at the city boundary neither the official nor the unofficial gifts were welcomed.

'Bread, salt and Bibles!' growled the Russian sergeant. 'All we want is a drink. Where can we get some vodka?'

The Wurmbrands realised they would have to use a more subtle approach.

The following day Richard was out with Mihai when they saw their first Russian couple — a captain and a woman sergeant. They were having difficulty over their shopping for they knew no Rumanian and the shopkeeper no Russian. Richard offered to interpret and helped them over their purchases. Although to Rumanians the Bucharest shops seemed depleted of goods after the prodigal luxury they had formerly displayed, to the Russians they seemed rich beyond belief. The woman wanted to buy some clothes and asked Richard if he could recommend a good store. He seized the opportunity for missionary work.

'I don't know much about ladies' clothes,' he said. 'Why don't you come to our house for lunch when you have finished your shopping and meet my wife. She will take you out this afternoon and show you the best dress shops.'

The couple were delighted and wrote down Richard's address, promising to be there within the hour. Little Mihai, however, was disappointed. Although only five, he took his father's duties as pastor very seriously.

'Father,' he demanded as the Russian pair departed. 'Why didn't you talk to them about God?'

'Do you remember, Mihai, when you planted that apricot stone?' his father replied. 'You kept digging it up to see if it had started to grow? Nothing happened, did it? Some things need patience. A kind invitation is a seed. It will grow.'

Mihai had a child's alert observation. He had clearly absorbed what his mother and father had said in his presence about the Russian sergeant the day before. Now as they walked home to the flat, he saw Russian soldiers coming out of wine shops with their arms full of looted bottles. Even to a child it was apparent that Russian soldiers liked to drink. Did his father think the Russian captain and the lady would also like to drink, he asked. So when the guests arrived, they had a glass of Mihai's wine and then sat down to their meal.

'First, we always say a grace to God in this house,' said Richard. He said the grace in Russian.

The guests put down their knives and forks. Would he say the words again? What did they mean? The girl recalled that her grandfather had had some 'holy books' but she had not read them because at school they were taught that religion was invented by the bourgeoisie to oppress the people.

Sabina never did take the woman sergeant shopping. Instead, all four of them spent the whole afternoon talking about Jesus. But it was not always easy; there was so little common ground between them.

Richard told them the parable of the man who had a hundred sheep and lost one and went in search of it. The Russians did not understand. 'How was it that he had a hundred sheep?' they asked. 'Why did he not send them to the collective farm?'

When Richard spoke of Jesus as king, the Russian reaction was 'Kings are bad men who tyrannise the people; this Jesus must have been a tyrant.'

When Richard told them the parable of the workers in the vineyard, they nodded their heads in approval. 'Those workers did well to rebel against the owner of the vineyard. It should have belonged to the collective.'

Richard very soon realised that to preach the Gospel to Russians after so many years of Communism, it was necessary to use different imagery from that in the New Testament. He would have to translate the Gospel into Marxist terms to make it comprehensible. It was something at times he despaired of achieving but eventually the Holy Spirit showed him the way.

Later he was able to publish pamphlets dealing with the relationship between Christianity and Marxism. He tried to make these books attractive to Communists by using their terms. For example, there were captions under the illustrations such as 'Jesus the Working Proletarian', 'Jesus driving the Capitalists out of the Temple'. Sometimes he and his colleagues published works which appeared at first sight to be pro-Communist. They had to do this in order to get the books past the censor. They would have such titles as 'Religion is the Opium of the People' and the first few pages would quote the sayings of Marx and Lenin. The censor, seeing this, would pass the book and, equally, Communists would begin to read it when it was given to them. Only by the time they had reached, say, page ten would they discover that the book was now all about Jesus — but by that time the Christian who had pressed it into their hands would be six streets away.

Even little Mihai played his part in the work of the Church, handing out Christian literature to the Communist troops. Russians love children and would often lift the little boy on to their knees and give him sweets. They would accept leaflets from a child where they might have been angry with an adult.

He was an intelligent child and listened to the talk of the grown-ups who flocked through the house. Already in his short life he had experienced more of tension and drama than many people ten times his age. Despite the pressing demands on his time, Richard always made time for his son, to teach him and tell him stories. Mihai accepted these stories at their face value — with some unexpected consequences.

One story that impressed him greatly was about a rich woman who, when asked for food by a beggar, gave him some mouldy cheese that she was going to throw away. The beggar did not care whether the cheese was mouldy or not; he was starving. So he was happy. The rich woman felt that she had done a good deed for the beggar, so she felt happy too. But that night she dreamed a dream. She was in heaven and there were tables spread with good things. Saints she recognised were sitting at the tables enjoying the food. She made to sit down with them herself but an angel directed her to a small table set apart on which was the piece of mouldy cheese she had given the beggar.

'This is your place,' said the angel. 'What you give, you get.'

Richard pointed out that this story illustrated what St. John meant when he said that a man who had two coats should give one 'to him that hath none'.

It so happened that after many years of 'making do', Richard had just been able to afford to buy himself a new suit.

'You have two suits,' said Mihai when the story was over. 'Now you must give one away!'

'Which shall I give?' asked Richard.

'The one you want to wear in heaven,' said Mihai. 'Old Mr. Ionescu must have your new one; then he can throw away that smelly old jacket he always wears.'

What could Richard do in the face of a child's direct logic? He had to make do with his old suit even longer.

The Wurmbrands had been utterly opposed to everything that Nazism stood for. They had seen and heard of dreadful crimes against humanity committed by German troops. Equally they had been opposed to Rumanian Fascists. Sabina in particular, having suffered the loss of her entire family, had particular reason to hate them. But now the Russians had arrived, these two groups were themselves defeated and in danger. Most of the German soldiers still in Rumania were victims of war, starving and terrified. Richard and Sabina could not deny them help, even though the penalty for concealing Germans was death. People used to

say: 'You are taking foolish risks for the sake of murderers'
but Richard would not agree. How many Rumanians, he
asked, would have had the courage to refuse to become Nazis
if Hitler had ruled in Rumania? Indeed, how many
Rumanians had supported the Iron Guard? And had there
not existed even in Germany many brave souls who had
helped Jews to escape? 'We must not hate a whole nation
because of its leaders,' he said. 'And God is always on the
side of the persecuted.' Love, the outpouring of a heart that
hates the sin but loves the sinner has always been the motive
power of Richard Wurmbrand's ministry.

Consequently, the Wurmbrand home became a refuge for
German soldiers on the run, just as, a few months previously,
it had sheltered Jews hunted by those same Germans. If God
made no distinction and allowed His rain to fall alike on the
just and the unjust, who was Richard to choose which persecuted people were most deserving of his help?

One German officer they were hiding asked Sabina: 'Why
do you, a Jewess, do this for me? When the German army
recaptures Bucharest, you will not find me helping you.'

Sabina replied: 'My family were killed by people like you,
but Jesus commands us to love our enemies. You yourself
admit to murdering Jews. I cannot absolve you of that sin;
only Jesus can do that. I will protect you if I can from the
police but I cannot protect you from the wrath of God.'

One day a group of *Blitzmädchen*, girls serving in the
German army, appealed to the Wurmbrands for sanctuary.
They were terrified of being deported to Russia. Someone
informed on them and soon Richard found the house surrounded by police.

Richard produced his identity card, issued under the Fascist régime. It had 'JEW' over-stamped on it in large capital
letters.

'Half our family have been murdered by the Nazis,' said
Richard. 'Do you think we would be likely to shelter
German girls?'

The police officer apologised and withdrew. 'The whole thing is obviously a mistake,' he said.

At the same time as they were providing sanctuary for hunted Germans, the Wurmbrands were also entertaining Russian troops and talking to them of Christ. There was a constant danger that the two would meet but, under God's providence, this never happened.

The Red soldiers were always stealing. One day two young men in uniform knocked on the Wurmbrands' door.

'Do you want to buy an umbrella?' they asked, offering three to choose from which Richard guessed were stolen.

'We are Christians in this house,' Richard replied. 'We don't buy; but we have something to give.'

He invited them in and Sabina brought them some milk to drink. One of the young men stared at her.

'Why, it was you who gave me the Bible,' he said.

'And you were the sergeant on the first tank into Bucharest,' cried Sabina in recognition.

The sergeant told them his name was Ivan. He still had the Bible in his locker at the barracks.

'I've read it,' he said, 'and, you know, it settled a question that was puzzling me. We have a Jew in our battalion. One of the older men, when he was drunk, used to rail at the Jew and say "You killed Christ". We all thought the chap was crazy. We'd all of us, not just the Jew, been killing people all the way from Stalingrad to Bucharest. We couldn't think why he should remember someone called Christ more than any of the others. But your Bible explained what the man was going on about.'

It seemed such a tragedy that anyone could reach Ivan's age without even having heard the name of Jesus. Later, he brought the Jew to the Wurmbrand home and Richard spent hours talking to them about the Bible, explaining everything from Genesis to Revelation. In due course, both young men became Christians. They visited the Wurmbrands frequently and thoroughly enjoyed being in a home instead of barracks. When the battalion was posted, Ivan brought a farewell present — a shining new electric fire. Richard and Sabina exchanged glances. They guessed that, like the umbrellas, it had been stolen — in gratitude for being shown the way of Christ! They sent the fire to a needy family who had been released from Auschwitz concentration camp. They felt Ivan would have approved.

Richard was appointed pastor first of the Swedish and afterwards of the Norwegian Mission to Israel in Bucharest. The Mission also had a Norwegian pastor named Solheim. Both men were asked to serve as representatives on the newly-formed World Council of Churches. One of their duties was to administer the relief funds sent from the west to aid famine-stricken Rumania. First Germany and now Russia had stripped and pillaged her resources. With wholesale conscription of all able-bodied men into the army, there had been left only the old or the maimed to till the land, and the agriculture had been sadly neglected.

Richard and Pastor Solheim distributed among the needy such clothes, money and food as they were able to obtain. They also turned the Mission into a canteen where they were able to give up to 200 people a day some little food to keep them from starving. They looked around for larger accommodation in order to extend their work. They succeeded in renting an enormous place from a once-wealthy Jewish doctor; one room was big enough for a ballroom. Richard and Sabina took a few rooms for their own use; the 'ballroom' (which could accommodate 200 people) became a church and the rest of the rooms were used by the Mission. The place was always filled with strange guests of differing nationalities and persuasions. Once again, no stranger was turned from the door and it was not unusual for thirty visitors to be sleeping there — in the hall, on the floor, sometimes even in the bath.

During 1945, after the war in Europe had ended, the Wurmbrand family grew overnight from one to seven! Richard and Sabina decided to foster six Jewish children released from concentration camps. There were thousands of little orphans like these, whose parents had been sent to the gas-chambers. The children were thin, haunted-looking and in rags but they soon began to laugh again in that loving house-hold. Mihai was delighted. 'You told me I couldn't have any brothers or sisters,' he said accusingly to his parents. 'Now I have three of each.'

Rumania had hoped that once the war was over and the last Germans had been driven from the country, the Rus-sians too would leave but this did not happen. Instead, the Communists imposed on Rumania a puppet Prime Minister called Groza. Young King Michael was powerless to oppose the growing Communist strength. One by one, the various Cabinet posts and Government positions were taken over by men loyal to Moscow. When the Communists were in com-plete control of the government, a Congress was convened of all Christian bodies. It was held in the Parliament building. Four thousand priests, pastors and ministers of all denomi-nations attended. Such was their fear of Communism, they elected Joseph Stalin as honorary president of the Congress! One after another, the delegates rose to their feet and de-clared it as their opinion that Christianity and Communism were fundamentally the same thing and could therefore work together. The proceedings were being broadcast and it seemed to the Wurmbrands who were at the Congress rep-resenting their Mission that to allow such statements to go out over the air was like spitting in the very face of Jesus.

'Richard,' urged Sabina. 'Stand up and wash away this shame from the face of Christ.'

'If I do,' he replied, 'you will lose your husband.'

'I don't want a husband who is a coward.'

It was wonderful that they were in complete accord on a matter that they knew was bound to have far-reaching consequences.

Richard sent up his card to the chairman with a request

to speak. The Communists were delighted at the prospect of a representative of the World Council of Churches making propaganda for them. Richard rose from his seat and made his way down the aisle to the platform. Every eye followed him and as he stepped up to the microphone a hush fell upon the hall. The atmosphere was tense with expectancy.

Richard began to speak. 'When the children of God meet,' he said, 'the angels also gather there to hear men praise the wisdom of God.'

They were all assembled in the hall, he continued, as representatives of their various churches and, as such, it was their duty to glorify God the Creator and Christ the Saviour, who died on the Cross. It was no part of their Christian duty to praise earthly powers that come and go, to align themselves with a system that denied the very existence of God.

The intensity of the listening in the hall could almost be felt. The platform party grew restless for the speeches from the Congress were being broadcast throughout Rumania. Suddenly the Minister of Cults, Burducea, jumped to his feet.

'Your right to speak is withdrawn!' he shouted.

Richard ignored him and went on. The audience began to applaud; Richard was saying all the things they had wanted to say but dare not.

'Cut that microphone,' bellowed Burducea, but his voice was drowned in the hubbub. The audience rose to their feet and clapped as Richard continued his defiant address. Finally someone cut the cable of the microphone and his voice could no longer be heard — but the audience had heard enough.

'*Pastorul! Pastorul!*' they chanted rhythmically as he made his way back to his seat. 'The Pastor! The Pastor!'

From that day on, Richard was no longer *a* pastor in Rumania; he had become *The Pastor* — shepherd of a very large and bewildered flock.

CHAPTER 5

The Church goes Underground

DESPITE RICHARD'S COURAGEOUS action at the Congress, many of the Church leaders yielded to Communism in the days that followed. One bishop had the hammer and sickle embroidered on his robes and asked his priests not to address him as 'Your Grace' any longer, but as 'Comrade Bishop'. Some priests became officers in the Secret Police. One high-ranking member of the Rumanian Lutheran Chruch began to teach that God had given three revelations: one through Moses, one through Jesus and the third through Stalin. The tragedy was that many of these Church leaders who collaborated with the Communists denounced those faithful pastors who refused.

Thus was founded the Underground Church in Rumania, a sort of secret society of the faithful whose aim was to evangelise, to preach the Gospel and, wherever possible, to win children for Christ.

In his capacity as pastor of the Swedish and Norwegian Missions and as a representative of the World Council of Churches in Rumania, Richard had the perfect cover for underground work. His official jobs gave him standing with the authorities but his main work now took two forms. One was to continue his help and ministry to the enslaved people of Rumania. The other was by secret means to bring the Good News of Christ to the million Russian soldiers who made up the army of occupation.

The Underground Church had to use all manner of ingenious methods to approach the Russians. Fortunately, they discovered that there were, just occasionally, Russian soldiers who were already secret Christians and these helped the work in many ways.

The Russian troops were eager for watches. They were evidently unable to buy them at home so that in Rumania they would acquire all they could lay their hands on, often by stealing. The jewellers' shops were soon empty and if a Rumanian whose watch had been stolen wanted to replace it, he had to go to the Russian barracks and buy one there. There were plenty available — sometimes Russian soldiers walked around the streets wearing several watches on each arm!

The members of the Underground Church spent a lot of time 'buying watches' — though their real purpose in visiting the barracks was, of course, to talk of Christ and to distribute pamphlets.

The first time Richard went was the day of the Feast of St. Peter and St. Paul. He spent a lot of time looking at watches the soldiers had for sale, until he had gathered quite a crowd round him. Then he casually asked: 'Is anyone here called Peter or Paul?'

One or two were.

'Do you know what day it is today?'

Thus he began to tell them about the two great saints. One of the soldiers, an older man, interrupted him.

'You haven't come here to buy a watch,' he said. 'You have come to speak of the faith. Pease tell us more, but do be careful.'

The man arranged that he would stand with his hand on Richard's shoulder. Every time he squeezed it, that would be a signal of danger and Richard would quickly start asking the price of watches again. When the pressure was released, he would carry on with his stories of Christ whom Peter and Paul had so lovingly served. This visit was repeated on other occasions and many of the Russian soldiers became Christians.

Some brave members of the Underground Church enrolled in the Secret Police in order to perform 'counter-espionage' on the Church's behalf. Some Christian doctors joined the Communist party for the sole purpose of gaining access to the prisons, in order to bring assistance and news to prisoners. Others deliberately took jobs in Government offices where they could be forewarned, perhaps, of Communist plans. By such means did the Underground Church survive but often these brave people had to endure the scorn and reproach of other Christians who thought they had gone over to the 'enemy' and abandoned their Christian faith.

All the Wurmbrand family were involved in the work of evangelism. Sabina discovered a talent for preaching and she began to hold street corner meetings, drawing large crowds. Indeed, on one occasion when speaking on the steps of the University, she was mistaken for the notorious Ana Pauker, the Rumanian Communist schoolteacher who had joined the Red Army and had executed her own husband for 'deviation' from Communist principles. No-one could understand why on this occasion at the University Comrade Pauker was urging her audience to repent of their sins!

Inevitably, it was only a matter of time before the King was deposed. He was the one political obstacle that remained between the Communists and complete control of Rumania. On December 30th, 1947, Groza presented him with an Instrument of Abdication and told him to sign it. The King refused. His palace was surrounded by Communist troops and once again he was told to sign. He was told he was an 'unsettling influence' and warned that if he did not abdicate he would be responsible for bringing bloodshed and civil war to his country. The King signed and the People's Republic of Rumania came into existence on that very day.

Mihai, who was almost nine, was very concerned when he heard what 'abdication' meant and realised that the handsome young King whose picture had disappeared from the wall of his classroom was actually going to be turned out of his palace. He knew that his father had had an audience with the King only shortly before.

'Why can't the King come and live with us?' Mihai demanded. He assumed that even Kings would automatically turn to The Pastor when in need.

'We have no room,' said Sabina. 'Our house is already full.'

'He could share my bed,' offered Mihai. 'It's a big one.'

'I don't think it would be big enough,' replied Richard. 'You see, the Queen Mother would have to come too, *and* all the Court. They would need sixty cars at least to get here. We couldn't ask the King without his courtiers.'

They could laugh over Mihai's innocent solution to the King's problems but it was laughter that was very near to tears. A fresh time of terror had begun. All opposition to Communism was being crushed without mercy. Hundreds and thousands of innocent people were 'liquidated' or thrown into prison for the sole crime of holding independent opinions. People became afraid to speak to each other in case they dropped an indiscreet word and were informed upon. Informers are at once the bane and the backbone of any Communist society. They were to be found all through the country from the highest offices of Government even down to the youngest classes in the schools. Even Mihai, young though he was, felt the tension of having to be careful what he said to his teachers or to the other children in his form.

He was sad, too, for his six 'brothers and sisters' had left. After the war was over, Russia had annexed the provinces of Bessarabia and Bukovina as part of the price Rumania had to pay for supporting Germany in the war. It was decided to re-populate these two provinces with refugees. Many orphans, like the Wurmbrands' foster-children, survivors from concentration camps, were being taken there. Richard and Sabina dreaded the thought of this happening to the children they had grown to love as if they were their own.

They hated the idea of their being brought up as Communists, indoctrinated with atheism.

An opportunity arose of sending the children to Palestine where the new State of Israel was coming into being. Here was a chance of a better life than in Bessarabia. It was an agonising decision; it was almost like parting with Mihai.

The children left aboard the Turkish steamer *Bulbul*, along with many other Jews bound for Palestine. Weeks passed but no news came of their arrival. Ships and planes of many nations joined in searching the Black Sea and the Eastern Mediterranean but no trace of the vessel was ever found. It was assumed that it had hit a wartime mine and gone down with all aboard. The ship never reached Israel and none of the passengers was heard of again.

Richard and Sabina were distraught with grief, though they tried to console themselves that the children had perhaps escaped a more lingering fate, for terrible things were being done in Rumania.

The Swedish and Norwegian Missions being active, were a prime target for the Communists. Organised gangs would attempt to shout Richard down when he went into the pulpit to speak, for he refused steadfastly to preach the Party line. Sometimes the hecklers would cause disturbances and fighting would break out in the church. On occasion, the opposition was so violent that Richard could only preach with a solid phalanx of his congregation guarding the pulpit.

Yet amongst all the violence and the terror, Richard and Sabina seemed to move unscathed. They had their work, their home, their friends, their little son. Richard had been imprisoned under the Fascist régime and beaten on more than one occasion but this was nothing compared with the sufferings some people endured. His work was difficult and dangerous but so far he personally was unharmed. How could he exhort others to bear their cross with forbearance when he himself carried so small a burden? This thought allowed him no peace. On many nights, he and Sabina prayed that they, too, might bear their cross for Christ.

Richard knew it was inevitable, particularly after his defiant speech at the Congress of Cults, that sooner or later he would be arrested. Even so, when the day came, he must have felt some inner turmoil beneath his outward calm. Yet the Secret Police were nonplussed by his firm handling of the situation. He would not go quietly with them, he said, unless the family was first allowed to pray and sing a hymn. He even suggested the Police sit down and listen!

All who were in the house knelt together in the room where the Police were waiting. What were Richard's thoughts then? Lord, is this the time of *my* testing? Is this where the cross begins? They sang a hymn, and Richard prayed and read one of the Psalms; then he went out quietly with his captors.

Two weeks went by. Three. That was as long as he had ever been detained under the Fascists. Four weeks. Five. Sabina was beside herself with anxiety. She approached everyone she could think of to help obtain Richard's release. At last, reluctantly, she once again approached the most powerful of their friends, the Swedish Ambassador to Rumania. Once again he took the unusual and undiplomatic step of interceding on behalf of a Rumanian national. After six weeks in prison Richard was released, but he guessed that this had only been a rehearsal for the ordeal that was to follow.

Friends urged him to leave the country. It was still possible, if difficult, to get away. It was tempting. Richard and Sabina talked about it over and over again. Richard was worried for his family. Was it fair to ask them to suffer? And could he not do more for the Underground Church if he went to the West? What purpose would it serve if he were in prison? The Mission would have to close. Pastor Solheim would not be allowed to stay on his own; he was a foreigner. And Richard might be put away for years. What good would it do to stay? And supposing Sabina were imprisoned as well? What would happen to Mihai?

One evening, when they had almost come to a decision to try to buy an exit visa, the words of Jesus came to them with great urgency: 'Whosoever will save his life shall lose it, and whosoever will lose his life for my sake shall find it.'

A day or two later, they were both at a secret meeting, in a private house. Some fifty or so were gathered in prayer. Suddenly a woman spoke out loud: 'One of you is thinking of leaving us but I say to you: "Remember that the good shepherd did not desert his flock. He stayed to the last." ' She had no knowledge that Richard and Sabina had been discussing flight but *they* knew Who had put the words into her mouth. They were to stay.

One Sunday morning in February of 1948, Richard left the house early promising to meet Sabina later at church. He never arrived. He just vanished from the streets.

CHAPTER 6

Kidnapped

RICHARD WAS IN PRISON.

When the cell door closed on him that Leap Year Day of 1948, he knew that he faced questioning, torture, perhaps years of imprisonment, even death. Yet he was not afraid.

It would be wrong to say that he was not anxious. The very thing had happened that he had feared when he had discussed with Sabina whether or not they should leave Rumania. Whatever must she be feeling now? When she found he was not at church, would she guess what had happened? Would she be told where he was being detained? Would she be able to visit him? And what of Mihai? He was only just nine — such a little boy to be deprived of his father. Had they after all been fair to him staying behind in Rumania when they had known surely that one day, like today, Richard would be arrested?

It would be equally wrong to say that he was not apprehensive. There was so much information inside his head that the Communists would like to know: names of workers, addresses of meeting places, secrets of the Underground Church. His enemies would stop at nothing to extract this information from him. Could he trust himself not to break down under stress and betray his friends?

Richard knew, without being told, that this was not going to be a mere six-week imprisonment. He had prepared himself for prison and torture as an athlete trains for a race. He had studied the lives of great Christian saints who had suffered for their faith and he had planned how he could adapt their experiences to his own.

Now the testing time had come.

He sat down on the plank bed and thought. February 29th. Leap Year Day. It had been a day of such bright promise when he had set out from home — was it so short a time ago? Then he remembered something. In the Bible, the words 'Don't be afraid!' occur 366 times. Not merely 365 times, once for each day of the year, but 366 times which would allow for Leap Year Day as well. And today *was* Leap Year Day. It was a coincidence that immediately cheered him.

Moreover, if God had made it so clear that he wanted Richard to stay in Rumania, then surely He would give him the strength to carry out whatever task it was He still wanted Richard to do.

Therefore, *he would not be afraid.*

There was nothing in the cell to help him pass the time, no books, no writing paper. The window was too high up in the wall to see out. There was nothing to do but think.

He thought about how he would cope with his interrogation when it came. They would be sure to make much of the fact that he was a pastor. Priests were always told: 'As a Christian you must tell us the whole truth about everything.' Yet what purpose would it serve if he betrayed his friends? It would not buy his own freedom, of that he was certain. He would be found guilty whatever he said. He decided that, if God would give him the strength to do it, he would try to leave his interrogators more confused by the end of an interrogation than they were at the beginning.

If there *were* an interrogation — that was the point. The Communists had their own methods; sometimes they would not ask any questions for a week. There was nothing to do. He just sat on his plank bed or paced up and down the narrow cell. He slept as much as the cold and his thin blanket would allow. Then one night at about ten o'clock, the cell door opened and he was told he was wanted for questioning. The guard made him wear dark goggles so that he could not see where he was going; it is unnerving to be led along unfamiliar corridors in the dark. Eventually he was pushed down onto a chair and the goggles were removed.

Richard blinked and turned his head, dazzled by a bright lamp directed straight into his eyes. The rest of the room was in shadow.

'Ah, Vasile Georgescu.' A voice from the shadows addressed Richard by the new name he had been given on his arrest. 'You will find paper and pen on that desk. Take your chair over there and write down about your life. We've brought you here to confess to us.'

Such a vague request. A confession. A confession of what?

Richard made up his mind that he did not care what he said about himself, provided he did not incriminate any of his friends and fellow-workers in the Underground Church. He wrote about his life as a boy and a young man. Then, in case the 'confession' might be read by Party leaders, he described how for many years he had been an atheist like themselves and what a sinful life he had led. That would surely attract their attention and make them read on! Then, at great length, he described the events and thinking that had brought him to a belief in God. He must have been writing for an hour or more before he was told he had done enough for that night and was led back blindfold to his cell.

He had expected that his 'confession' would be followed by questioning on the following day but he was to learn over the years that the communists did not work like that. They were artists in interrogation, using every psychological device to break down their victim's resistance. It was like a refined game of cat and mouse. They used not to tell a prisoner anything. He did not know why he was in prison or when he was to be tried. If he confessed, was he confessing to the right crime? What did they want to know? There would be long delays between interviews so that the prisoner became nervous, starting every time he heard footsteps in the corridor outside his cell. Were they coming for him now? The prisoner would be in a constant state of tension and uncertainty. There were other tricks to strain his nerves. He would be told the date of his trial, and then it would be postponed at the last minute, just when he had nerved himself to endure the strain of it. He would hear the screams of prisoners, the sound of a firing-squad, and would not know whether it was real or whether it was a tape-recording. Then there would be silence. And time — unending, uninterrupted time. Time to think, time to worry, time to panic.

So once again it was several days before Richard had his second interview — in a basement room this time, just to make it more difficult and confusing to reach blindfolded. There was no ill-treatment — just questioning, going through his statement line by line and asking him to give further details. But at intervals his interrogator would shoot a question at Richard that had nothing to do with his statement hoping to catch him off his guard. He could never be sure when one of these questions was coming and had to watch carefully everything he said in case he should let slip an indiscreet word.

Richard's next inquisitor read from a typed list of questions. 'Write down the names of everyone you know.'

That was going to need care. There were friends Richard wanted to shield but if he did not put down enough names, his questioners would know his list was false. He thought for a moment, then started by writing down all the names of people openly and legitimately associated with him: Sabina and Mihai, Pastor Solheim at the Mission, the church officials, the caretaker and so on. He went on to write down the names of as many Communist members of parliament as he could remember, of known informers and the like. Any names that were safe, provided he could keep on writing.

This type of questioning went on for months, all part of a wearing down process before moving on to the next stage of interrogation. Often, after a period of weeks, Richard would find they were asking the same questions all over again and he would rack his brains to remember how he had answered the first set of questions; otherwise he would face yet further inquisition because the answers were different.

He was encouraged when the prison barber whispered to him that Sabina was well and carrying on Richard's work. It gave him a wonderful surge of thankfulness for he had been desperately anxious lest Sabina also should have been arrested and Mihai left to starve or to rely on the charity of neighbours. It gave him strength to know they were safe.

Richard could not know how frantic was Sabina's search for news of him. When he first disappeared, she had convinced herself that he had met someone in need and had maybe gone to their house and become so involved in their problem that he had forgotten the time. Then she had phoned or visited all the hospitals. No, no-one following Richard's description had been brought into the casualty ward. With a sense of foreboding, she tried the prisons. The officials looked down their lists. 'Wurmbrand? There is no-one of that name here.' She went from one department to another in the Ministry of the Interior. People opened filing cabinets. Looked through official-looking folders. 'Wurmbrand? No-one of that name in our records.'

It was rumoured that Richard had been taken to Moscow. Sabina could not, would not believe that this was true. Every evening she laid his place at the table. Surely he would come tonight; he had never been held for more than a few weeks before.

In despair she appealed to the Swedish Ambassador again. Perhaps he could at least find out something definite. He tried. It was eventually to lose him his post as Ambassador, but he tried. He went to the very highest level and asked Rumania's Foreign Minister, Ana Pauker. She had her answer ready: 'Our information is that Pastor Wurmbrand has absconded with the money entrusted to him for relief work. He is not in the country.'

It was many, many months before Sabina had any news, and then only after wasting enormous sums of money in bribes. One day a man came to the Mission saying he had met Richard.

'I'm a warder,' he said. 'Don't ask me which prison, but I take him his food. He said you'd pay me well for a bit of news.'

'How much do you want?'

The sum he named was exorbitant. If Sabina paid, she would have practically nothing left. She turned to Pastor Solheim. 'What shall I do?'

The pastor was doubtful. The man reeked of *ţuica*, the fiery plum brandy of Rumania. How much could such a man be relied on? Solheim fetched a bar of chocolate from the relief stores.

'Give this to Pastor Wurmbrand,' he said, 'and bring back a message in his handwriting on the wrapper. Then we will pay you what you ask.'

A few days later the man was back. He took off his cap and carefully extracted a piece of paper from the lining. It carried a single line of writing but in Richard's unmistakable hand: 'Dearest wife. I thank you for your sweetness. I am well. Richard.'

That was all — twelve words on the wrapper of a chocolate bar — but they were more precious and beautiful to Sabina than the greatest love poem ever written.

She needed news if only to sustain her for she was suffering greatly. It took all her Christian faith to rely on Christ's promise: 'Be not anxious for the morrow.'

Men from the Living Space Office came to look over the house. 'You have too much accommodation,' they said. 'And a ten-year-old boy does not need a room to himself.'

So Mihai had to move into one room with his mother while the rest of the house was taken over by a captain in the Security Police. Private property had been confiscated by the State so Sabina had now to pay her rent to the government instead of to the doctor. It was hard to find the rent. She had no income of her own, her small savings had long since been exhausted on bribes, and she could not get work because she was the wife of a political prisoner.

'But it has been denied by the highest authorities in the land that my husband is in prison!'

'That is nothing to do with us. You cannot have a job anyway because you have no ration card.'

Sabina trailed round to the department that issued ration cards.

'No ration card for you,' she was told. 'You have no job. We only issue ration cards to workers.'

'But how am I to live? I have a little son.'

'That's your worry.'

So Sabina had to earn money where she could, and jobs that could be done without a work card were very poorly paid — there were so many people after them. Miraculously, each day her needs were met. There was never anything over, there was not always enough, but there was *something*. 'Be not anxious for the morrow.'

It was as well Richard knew nothing of this; he was struggling with a dreadful decision. He had made up his mind that if he was tortured, he would take his own life rather than betray others. The problem was how to do it. The guards checked the prisoners and their cells regularly for any possible means of suicide — slivers of glass, nails, a razor blade, a length of string. One day a solution to his problem suggested itself to Richard. He had hardly slept at all for a week so when the doctor came on his rounds Richard asked him for sleeping pills. He was so dazed with lack of sleep, he said, that he was becoming confused and could not remember the correct answers to the questions put to him in his now daily interrogation. The doctor prescribed one sleeping tablet each night and the guard would look into his mouth to make sure he had taken it. But Richard managed to conceal the pill under his tongue. By the end of a month, he had thirty pills hidden in a small slit in the seam of the palliasse on the other bed in his cell.

Thirty pills would surely be enough to end his life if he were in danger of breaking down. The thought of the little hoard in the mattress gave him strength when he faced his interrogators, but it made him depressed when he was alone.

It was summer. He could hear sometimes in his cell faint sounds from the world outside — the clang of a tramcar, a girl's voice singing. Once he heard a woman's voice calling to her children. 'Emil! Silviu! Come here!' and his heart ached for Sabina and Mihai. Once a feathery seed drifted in through the cracked window pane and settled on the floor. He remembered Mihai's apricot seed, and the Russian couple in the shop, and the luncheon party with the bottle of wine. He had told Mihai: 'An invitation is a kind of seed. It will grow.'

What was God doing? If He had put it into Richard's heart to sow seeds of love for Christ, why was He allowing him to end his life before he had finished sowing? An answer to this reproach came promptly. The following morning, a guard came into the cell and picked up the palliasse with the hoarded pills.

'We want this for another prisoner,' he said.

Richard's first reaction was anger that all his careful deception to obtain the pills had been wasted; then he laughed and felt calmer than he had done for weeks.

If God so clearly did not want his suicide, then He would assuredly give Richard strength to face what lay ahead.

CHAPTER 7

Joy of the Cross

COLONEL DULGHERU, grand inquisitor of the Secret Police, sat behind his desk. His hands, small and delicate as a woman's, drummed lightly on the papers in front of him.

'You've been playing with us, Georgescu,' he said, indicating the sheets covered with Richard's handwriting. 'We have been patient with you long enough. Now we want results.'

He began to question Richard about a Red Army man caught smuggling Bibles into Russia. It was a new line of interrogation. Up to now all the questions had been about Richard's contacts with the West, about his work as a pastor, nothing about his mission to the Russians. The captured soldier was, in fact, a man Richard had himself baptised. Perhaps a tiny hesitation on Richard's part made Dulgheru suspect that at last he was on to something important.

That night, both plank beds were taken out of Richard's cell and he was given only a hard upright chair on which to rest. Every few minutes he heard the metallic click of the shutter to the peephole in his door and knew that he was being watched. If he dozed off for a moment balanced on the chair, the guard would come in and kick him awake. The process was repeated night after night for several weeks until he lost all sense of time. Once his confused brain thought he heard Sabina screaming in the next cell. Was it really she, or was it a nightmare? In his exhaustion, he could not distinguish dream from reality. Dulgheru would come to the cell in the middle of the night and continue his questioning there but on no occasion, despite the mental torture, could the colonel extract answers that were of any use to him.

'Don't you realise,' he screamed one night in exasperation, 'that I have the power to have you executed, now, this very night?'

Richard still had the strength to say to him: 'Colonel, let us try an experiment. I know you can have me shot as you say, but put your hand on my heart. If you can feel it fluttering, you will know that what I have said is all lies and there is no God. I shall be afraid of dying. But if my heart is beating calmly, you will know that I am not afraid. That is because I know there *is* a God, that there *is* an eternal life. I know that if you have me shot, I shall go straight to my Lord.'

Dulgheru struck Richard across the face.

'All right,' he shouted. 'You've asked for it. Tomorrow you'll meet Comrade Brinzaru.'

Major Brinzaru was the prototype torturer of the spy film — large, brutal, with hairy arms like a gorilla and ugly yellow teeth. He showed Richard the tools of his trade — clubs, coshes, whips. He picked up a rubber truncheon and tested it lovingly, as a man might try a favourite golf club. He showed Richard the trade mark: 'Made in U.S.A.'

'Your American friends give us the tools,' he grinned. 'We do the job.'

Then he locked Richard up in his cell again to think over what he had seen. Strangely, Richard never had the beating from Brinzaru. That night as he was resting on his hard chair, the spy-hole in the door flicked open and Brinzaru called through the opening: 'Still there, Georgescu? What's your Jesus doing tonight?'

'He's praying for you,' said Richard.

Richard's first physical torture took place on the following day. He was made to stand with his arms raised above his head, finger-tips touching the cold plaster of the wall.

'Just keep him like that,' Brinzaru said to the guard.

Richard stood in that position for hours, till his arms and legs were numb. When he collapsed to the floor in a faint, he was revived with a sip of water and made to stand facing the wall again. Guard relieved guard, day after day, night after night, and still Richard stood, arms above his head, facing the wall. His legs were swollen, his arms were like leaden weights. The pain was excruciating. The wall seemed to loom over him.

That way lay madness.

He decided to concentrate on walls that were mentioned in the Bible. He thought of the verse in Isaiah which said that Israel's wrongdoing had put a wall between God and his people. That verse saddened him. The Christian Church had not been vigilant. It had allowed Communism to grow and spread.

He remembered the phrase: 'With my Lord, I leap over the wall.' That verse gave him hope. God would sustain him.

He thought about the walls of Jericho coming down, about the walls of Jerusalem rising up. He murmured to himself over and over again a verse from the Song of Solomon: 'My beloved is like a roe or a young hart; behold, he standeth behind our wall.' He tried to picture Jesus standing behind him, holding him up, supporting his arms as Moses' arms were supported on the mountain top until the Israelites had won the victory. As long as he could concentrate his mind on something, Richard could bear the pain.

From time to time, Major Dulgheru looked in on him to see whether he was prepared to 'co-operate' and say how the Bibles were being smuggled into Russia. When he had no success, Dulgheru decided to change the treatment.

'Put your shoes on. Walk!' ordered the guard.

Richard fumbled to force his swollen feet into his shoes but they would no longer fit. 'Come on. Hurry. Keep going round. Walk!'

Four paces down the cell. A wall. Turn. Two paces across the cell. A wall. Turn. Four pages up the cell. A wall. Turn. Two paces across the cell. A wall. Turn. Round and round and round.

'Halt! Turn about! Walk. *Keep walking!*'

Round and round and round.

Four paces up the cell. A wall. Turn. Two paces across the cell. A wall. Turn. Four paces down the cell. A wall. Turn. Two paces across the cell. A wall. Turn. Round and round and round.

'Faster!'

Hour after hour. Day after day. Night after night. Round and round and round. If he stumbled and fell, the guards dragged him to his feet and clubbed him till he started again. Round and round and round. His feet bled, his legs sagged. He clung to the walls while the guards screamed at him. He crawled on all fours. Round and round and round.

At last, through the agony and the exhaustion, Richard forced himself to pray for the guards. And after that it seemed that the cell was moving round him, not he round the cell.

There were other tortures. Richard was trussed like a chicken for the oven and hung upside down while the soles of his feet were beaten; he was whipped; he was branded with red hot irons; other things were done to him which are too unspeakable to record. All the time he was urged to talk, to co-operate, to confess.

After weeks of this treatment, Richard gave in. He would sign any confession they wanted *about himself*. He admitted to adultery, to homosexuality, to theft of the church bells (his church had no bells but what did that matter?). He admitted to spying and treachery. What harm could such confessions do to him? God knew he was innocent.

He was asked for the names of his accomplices. He wrote a long list, with addresses. At least it would gain him a night's rest, without interruption. Brinzaru was delighted. The list might earn him promotion.

A few days later, Richard was flogged again. Brinzaru had checked the list. All the people on it were either already dead or safely out of Rumania!

During all his years in prison, Richard never once betrayed anyone. By fixing his mind on Christ, he found that even the most ghastly treatment could be borne. If anything, it seemed to bring him nearer to Christ. When he was flogged, Richard would remember that Jesus was flogged and would rejoice to share His pain. When he was mocked, he realised that the mockery Jesus endured could well have been far worse than His crucifixion.

Richard had prayed for a chance to bear a cross for Christ and his petition had most surely been granted. It is not easy to understand how such agony could become bearable but Richard was now discovering the truth of the promise Christ had spoken to him eleven years before in that village in the Carpathians:

'Do not fear the Cross! You will find it the greatest of joys!'

CHAPTER 8

In Solitary Confinement

IT WAS OCTOBER 1948 and the beginning of winter. Already there would be snow in the mountains. In the Calea Rahovei, the prisoners shivered. Their frugal diet and tattered clothing gave them nothing to withstand the cold.

The door of Richard's cell opened and the guard brought in a plate of goulash — piled high, hot and savoury and steaming. With it were four whole slices of bread. There was more food than Richard normally had in a week. Tears of joy trickled down his cheeks as he picked up his spoon; but before he could eat even one mouthful the guard opened the door again.

'No time for food now. Bring your things. You're moving to a new prison.'

It was yet another refinement of torture.

Richard's new prison was *underneath* the Ministry of the Interior which is a handsome building much admired by tourists visiting Bucharest. They would be appalled if they knew what lay beneath their feet. Mihai must have walked hundreds of times across the square outside the Ministry, unaware that his father was thirty feet below him.

Richard's new cell was three paces by three. Being underground, the only air came through a tube in the ceiling. A naked electric light bulb burned day and night. There was no window, no furniture except for the familiar plank bed and straw pallet. There was not even the usual bucket in the corner. He would have to ask the guard when he wanted to use the latrines.

That was another carefully calculated horror inflicted on prisoners. The guard would be too busy and the prisoner had to wait. Or he would deliberately not hear the prisoner when he begged and implored to be taken from his cell for relief. It was a pain to contain oneself, an agony and a humiliation to soil oneself. Some prisoners went without their scanty food and drink rather than suffer this particular torment.

Richard's biggest trial was the silence.

No sounds from the outside world filtered down to his tomb-like cell. There was not even the familiar clatter of boots in the corridor, the clanging of cell doors that he had known in his other prison. Here the guards wore soft shoes. The cell doors moved smoothly on well-oiled hinges. No-one spoke to a prisoner. His meals — bread and watery soup — were placed silently on the floor. Instructions were given by gesture. The prisoner's only chance of conversation was when he was interrogated.

Richard had never been the sort of priest who devoted hours to meditation. He was a man of action. He preached with urgency. He loved people, overwhelming their doubts about Christ by the sheer enthusiasm of his own faith. Now he would have no props to that faith, no admiring congregation, no dramatic conversions, no underground mission to stimulate him with its dangers. He had no-one but God. How real was his Christianity now?

As the months went by in that silent, underground cell, he had many bad moments. Most of these were when his mind dwelt on what could happen to Sabina and Mihai. Had she been persuaded to divorce him? Was she in prison? One day his control snapped and he beat wildly on the cell door shouting: 'What have you done with my son? What have you done with my son?' He screamed the words over and over again until the guards rushed in and held him down on the bed and gave him an injection that silenced him into blessed unconsciousness. There were times when the cell was thronged with all the people he had ever injured in his life, provoking memories of sins he had hoped were done with for ever.

But these were the bad times. God showed him how to find a strength within himself.

He worked out a routine. It was possible to distinguish between day and night by the visits of the warders with food. As soon as he was sure he would not be disturbed any more for several hours, he began a time of prayer.

He went over his day, thanking God that he was still alive, expressing his gratitude for any small detail that might have distinguished that day from any other day. He reviewed his life, his work, his marriage, pouring out his gratitude for the many blessings he had received, confessing everything he could now recognise as a fault. Few men can have examined their souls more searchingly.

Then he would preach a sermon as if to his congregation, beginning 'Dear Brethren' and ending with 'Amen', just as he would have done in his church. They were not always good sermons. He had no paper to make notes, no books to enrich his mind. He had to struggle to remember his Bible. Sometimes he got the verses wrong or the books mixed up. Other times he could not remember anything at all from the Bible but he struggled to finish his sermon, no matter how bad it was.

Among the most precious moments of his nightly programme were the times when he sent out thoughts to Sabina and listened in his heart for her reply. They really did communicate in this way. Sabina has herself recorded how she would lie in bed and *know* that Richard was thinking of her and would send her thoughts winging back to him with the message 'I love you'.

Sometimes Richard would pretend he was Colonel Dulgheru and would try to understand why he was as he was, what pressures *he* had to withstand, what *his* fears were. He, too, was a prisoner — of the system that now held Rumania in its grip. That way Richard would find it easier to pray for him. Then he would try to look at himself as he imagined Colonel Dulgheru would look at him. That also helped. It even enabled him to pray for his torturers.

His thoughts turned to dancing, how in many countries it was used as a form of worship. He recalled how David 'danced before the Lord'. He remembered a word of Jesus: 'Blessed are you when men come to hate you, when they exclude you from their company and reproach you and cast out your name as evil on account of the Son of Man. Rejoice in that day and leap for joy.' The first part of that verse was true of him, even to the 'casting out of his name'. Did anyone in this place know he was Richard Wurmbrand and not Vasile Georgescu? If the first half of the verse could be so appropriate, he would make the other half right also.

So Richard danced — as much as anyone could dance in a cell three paces square — leaping about the room like a madman. The first time he did it, the guard really did think he had gone mad. It was one of the guard's duties to watch for signs that a prisoner's mind was beginning to crack under the strain of imprisonment, for if he went to pieces a prisoner would be of no more use for questioning. So the guard rushed off to his canteen and came back with a hunk of bread and some cheese and sugar, and broke the rule of silence as he tried to soothe this strange, laughing, capering figure. Richard ate the food gratefully, and remembered that the *complete* verse in St. Luke's Gospel that had prompted his dancing ran: 'Rejoice in that day and leap for joy — *for behold, your reward is great*'.

It was a very large hunk of bread, far more than he usually had in a whole week!

Thereafter Richard tried to dance some part of every day. He did not receive any more cheese or sugar or bread but the activity cheered him and helped to keep his body less *un*-healthy. The guards soon became used to his queer antics.

So the months passed and Richard disciplined himself to cope with the boredom and the silence. It was no longer boring or silent for him. God was very close.

During the daytime Richard used to play himself at chess, using chessmen made of crumbs of bread pounded together with scrapings of distemper off the wall. Thus he could play black bread versus not-so-black bread. Eventually he found someone to share his game.

One night he heard faint tapping on the wall beside his bed. There was someone in the next cell. He returned the tapping. Gradually, he and his fellow-prisoner worked out a laborious code of tapping so that they could communicate with each other. The man told him he had been a radio engineer before he was arrested. Over the weeks that followed he taught Richard the Morse code. By this means they played chess together and eventually were able to converse quite fluently. The tapping went on from cell to cell throughout the prison. New prisoners came. Incredible though it seems, the Morse code enabled Richard to preach the gospel through the wall, to hear confessions and to turn people to Christ!

One morning when his then neighbour had reminded him that the day was Good Friday, Richard searched around in the lavatory for something sharp and found a nail. He scratched the name 'JESUS' on the wall of his cell. So small a sign might bring comfort to some wretched prisoner who came after him. Needless to say, the word was discovered and as punishment Richard was put in the 'carcer'. This was a sort of upright coffin spiked on the inside with nails. It was all right provided its occupant kept perfectly still but, should he sway or sag — as was inevitable after several hours — the nails lacerated his body. Some prisoners had to endure the carcer for a week but Richard was only confined for two days. The prison doctor had warned the authorities that his health was in a dangerously low condition. He was emaciated and scarred and coughing constantly. His tuberculosis had returned and he really needed drugs and good food, fresh air and skilled nursing.

One day when the prisoners' latrines were blocked, he was taken to those used by the guards. There was a mirror over the washbasin and he saw himself for the first time for two years. Long confinement without any daylight had made him like a plant kept too long in the dark. His hair was thin and lank, his face pallid, the skin drawn tight over the cheek-bones. His always deepset eyes were sunk even deeper in their sockets. He looked an old man, yet he was still only forty ... forty-one ... forty-two? How long had he been in this place where there was no time? Would anyone recognise him now as the handsome Pastor Wurmbrand?

One of his interrogators was a young lieutenant called Grecu. He pushed over a pen and paper and ordered Richard to write down the names of all the people who had communicated with him in prison.

'We know you are tapping out messages to each other. Write down what these messages say and who says them.'

He went out of the room.

It was two years since Richard had held a pen in his hand. He could hardly form the letters on the paper.

'I am a disciple of Christ,' he wrote, 'Who has taught us to love our enemies. I pray daily for all Communists, that they may be converted and become my brothers. I cannot reveal to you what other prisoners have said. That is between them and God.'

Richard put down the pen and waited. Grecu returned, picked up the paper and read what had been written. He was silent for some time, then he turned a troubled face to Richard.

'Why do you say you love *me*?' he asked.

They had many discussions after that, under the guise of 'interrogation', but the information Grecu was seeking was the sort Richard was only too glad to give him — the message of God's love and mercy. Two weeks later, Lieutenant

Grecu in his Security Officer's uniform came to Richard in his patched prison rags and began to talk about his own sins against God and his fellow men.

Thereafter, for a short time, the burden of the prisoners was lightened in a number of tiny ways. Grecu still had to give lip service to the Communist party and it was dangerous and difficult to do anything for prisoners without its being noticed. But to a prisoner, even a kind glance is like water in a thirsty land.

It did not last long. One day Grecu disappeared. For all Richard knew, he could well now himself be in a cell beneath the Ministry of the Interior.

CHAPTER 9

Room Four

RICHARD WAS IN solitary confinement for nearly three years before he was tried. Towards the end of that time, he was very near death. The T.B. was markedly worse; now he brought up blood whenever he coughed.

'We're not murderers like the Nazis,' Colonel Dulgheru said to him. 'We want you to live — and suffer.'

Judging by their determination to keep him alive but still hidden, the Communists must have set great store on Richard's importance to them. He was moved by night to the prison hospital of Vacaresti, a converted monastery on the outskirts of Bucharest. Even though he was so weak that he had to be carried to the ambulance on a stretcher, it was wonderful to see the moon and stars again.

Before being lifted into the hospital, his head was wrapped in a sheet lest he be recognised. He was put in a separate cell from the rest of the hospital inmates. No-one was allowed to see him except the prison doctor and then only with a guard present. Richard was too weak to leave his bed. Often he tossed in delirium, but there were lucid moments when he could look through the small window and see the sky. No longer was he cocooned in the silence of his underground cell. Here he could hear a bird singing. There was joy, too, in that his guard was a secret Christian. There was little the man dare do to ease Richard's lot — warders had been sentenced to as much as twelve years merely for giving an apple or a cigarette to a prisoner — but it was like a blessing to Richard even to be able to hear the name of Christ whispered in his ear.

His trial, if such it could be called, took place in one of the rooms of the hospital. By the time he had stumbled along corridors with a sheet over his head and a soaring temperature, he needed an injection before he could even sit upright to listen to the proceedings. His judges were four men and one woman.

'A lawyer has been nominated to defend you,' he was told by the President of the court. 'He has waived your right to call witnesses.'

The prosecutor gave a long catalogue of Richard's alleged crimes: spy work through the World Council of Churches, spreading imperialist ideology, infiltrating the Party . . . The accusations meant nothing to him. The room whirled. He was slipping into unconsciousness again. Another injection revived him. His defence lawyer was on his feet. They had been given no opportunity to speak together but that did not matter; there was nothing the lawyer could say. He was only there to make a pretence of justice.

'Have you anything to say?' demanded the President.

'I love God,' murmured Richard as the room blurred round him.

He was just conscious enough to hear his sentence, twenty years' hard labour. Then he was hooded with the sheet and dragged back to his bed. The trial had taken ten minutes.

Shortly afterwards, he was taken to the prison at Tirgul-Ocna, a small town in the foothills of the Carpathians some two hundred miles north of Bucharest. The train journey took two days. There were some forty men and women in the goods wagon with Richard, all of them sick with tuberculosis; all, like Richard, wearing fifty-pound chains riveted round their ankles.

It was cheering to find that his new prison doctor was an old family friend, Dr. Aldea — a prisoner like himself but allowed to practise medicine among his fellows.

'I won't deceive you,' he said after examining Richard thoroughly. 'You have about two weeks to live. Try to eat what you can. The food here isn't good but it is better than nothing.'

Richard was moved into a bed in Room 4. That in itself was a sentence of death. Only the hopeless medical cases went there. No-one had ever left Room 4 except to be put in his grave.

For two weeks Richard hovered on the brink of death. He coughed up blood and pus, his body ran with sores. Dr. Aldea had no drugs to offer him; there was no nursing of any kind. Slightly less sick prisoners attended to the needs of those who could not help themselves, but they could do little for Richard except give him sips of water when he choked and turn him on his side when he groaned.

But after the two weeks had gone by, he was still clinging to life.

Room 4 contained twelve beds. It was quiet but not silent. When men know they are dying, they have no time to quarrel; they need their companions for comfort and assurance. No warders disturbed the peaceful fellowship of Room 4 because there were no warders. None was prepared to run the risk of being infected with T.B. All chores were done by prisoners from the other wards.

Richard spent two years in Room 4, from 1951 to 1953, not the two weeks Dr. Aldea had predicted. He saw scores of men die, some quickly, some after lingering illness, but all of them at peace. Some men who were brought in were 'intellectuals' like himself, some were former Fascists, others were Communists already the victims of their own party. There were saints and sinners, landowners and peasants, priests and criminals. Many were declared atheists, yet not one of them died without feeling the need to make his peace with God. If Richard had had no other evidence, if he had had no experience of his own to justify his faith, this fact alone would have compelled him to believe that God exists.

Richard had been sentenced to twenty years' hard labour but the first two years he spent at Tirgul-Ocna he was rarely strong enough even to leave his bed. After the years of solitary confinement, it was wonderful to enjoy fellowship with other men.

There was old Filipescu who would recite long passages of Shakespeare. He had been a revolutionary since 1907.

'Pah!' he would say scornfully of the present Communist administration. 'I suffered for Socialism before any of them were born.'

But Socialism is not Communism, so Filipescu was in prison.

There was Moisescu, a small, middle-aged Jew who had been persecuted in the anti-Semitic days of the Iron Guard and the German occupation. When the Iron Guard lost their power and the Russian Army drove out the Germans, Moisescu bought up all the stocks of green shirts he could lay hands on, with a view to dyeing them blue and re-selling them at a profit. That way he could make capital out of his persecutors. But before he could finish all the dyeing, his house was searched and the green shirts were found. Although he was a Jew, he was accused of supporting the Fascists! So Moisescu was in prison.

The courage of the prisoners was heartening. Men who had suffered all manner of tortures could still hope, could still make wry jokes about their torturers.

'Have you heard the one about Hell?' they would ask. 'A Communist and a Capitalist both died and went to Hell. When they got there they found there were two entrances. One was marked "Communist Hell"; the other was marked "Capitalist Hell". They were both very afraid of suffering hell-fire so they decided to sink their differences. They discussed at length which entrance to use. In the end the Communist won the argument. "You come into my Hell," he said. "It's bound to be better in there for it's always the same under Communism: when there are matches, there's no coal; when there is coal, there are no matches; when there are both coal and matches, the furnace breaks down!"'

'Who were the first Communists?' asked a farmer named Aristar.

'You tell us,' said the rest of the ward.

'Adam and Eve,' came the reply. 'And why? Because they had no clothes, no house, they had to share the same apple — and still thought they were in paradise!'

Jokes and stories helped the time to pass, took men's minds off the pain of their illness. Richard, when he had the strength, told dozens of stories. He told the parables of Jesus which many of them had never heard. He gave the old stories new settings to fit the prisoners' own conditions, bringing wonder and hope into many an empty heart.

Prisoners from other wards sometimes came to Room 4 with small gifts to comfort the dying. At Easter a friend brought a small twist of paper to a patient named Gafencu.

'It's been smuggled in. Go on! Open it!' he said.

Eleven pairs of eyes from the other beds watched while Gafencu's fingers fumbled to open the screw of paper. There were gasps of wonder. Inside the paper were two shining white lumps of sugar. Such luxury had not been seen by any of them for years. Gafencu carefully wrapped up the lumps of sugar and put them by his bedside.

'Thank you,' he said to his friend, 'but I shall not eat them yet. Someone may be worse off than I am during the day.'

A few days later Richard's condition deteriorated and he was again on the brink of death. The sugar passed from bed to bed till it was in Richard's hands.

'Do take it,' Gafencu whispered across the ward 'as a gift from me.'

Richard thanked him but he did not eat the sugar either. Someone else's need might be greater. For two years the sugar passed round Room 4, twice coming back to Richard, but every man who received it saved it for someone worse off than himself.

Each new batch of prisoners arriving at Tirgul-Ocna

brought snippets of news from the outside world. To the occupants of Room 4 it seemed that life inside their prison was no worse than life outside in so-called freedom! But their cheerful resignation was soon to come to an end.

For some time, rumours had spread through the prison of a new and frightening form of 're-education' of prisoners — a polite word for beating-up and even viler treatment. Some prisoners under threat of torture had agreed to swear allegiance to the Communist party and were formed into an organisation called the P.C.C. or 'Prisoners with Communist Convictions'. The P.C.C. were put in charge of the 're-education' programme. Terror gripped Tirgul-Ocna. The P.C.C. went mad in their brutality and inhumanity. The things they did to prisoners are too nauseating to record — and they brought the required results. Prisoners who had stood up to months of interrogation broke down under the attentions of the P.C.C. and denounced wives, parents and friends. Desperation led the prisoners to revolt. Even Richard approved the planned demonstration.

'Jesus was a fighter when the situation demanded it,' he said. 'He was not always meek and mild like the figures in religious paintings. He drove the merchants from the temple with a whip.'

The demonstration was planned for May 1st, 1952. On this day, Labour Day, the birth of Communism was celebrated with a holiday. The inhabitants of the town of Tirgul-Ocna always had a football match in the stadium next to the prison. Soon after the game began, there was a crash of broken glass as prisoners smashed their windows. They hammered on metal mugs and plates, they shouted 'Help us! Help us!' 'We are bring tortured here!' 'Your fathers and sons and brothers are being murdered!' The football match was abandoned and crowds gathered outside the prison. However, no protest by weak and unarmed prisoners could last for long against guards lashing out with rifle butts. The prison became quiet; the crowds dispersed. At

Tirgul-Ocna, the régime was stiffened but merci- fully — perhaps because news of the demonstration spread throughout the country — there were no reprisals.

Each new prisoner had some different story to tell of the oppression and misery under which Rumania laboured. One account that particularly shocked Room 4 was that given by Abbot Iscu of his experiences in the slave camp on the Danube–Black Sea Canal at Poarta Alba.

The Danube rises in the Black Forest in Germany and flows for 1,740 miles before it reaches its outlet in the Black Sea. For many miles it forms the boundary between Bulgaria and Rumania but when it is only forty miles from the coast, it turns north and then east, meandering for three hundred miles across Rumania's Dobrudja plain. The river's delta covers a thousand square miles of marshland, a vast wilder- ness of reeds and dwarf trees, threaded by innumerable shal- low waterways. There are few human settlements here. The area is the haunt of wolves, wild boar and otters; of pelicans, flamingos and egrets; of whooper swans and sacred ibis. There is, accordingly, no major port at the mouth of the Danube.

In 1949 a vast project was put in hand to cut a ship-canal through to the Black Sea from the point where the river swings northwards. Engineers warned that the river did not carry a sufficient volume of water at this point to supply a canal as well as the river's natural channel. The engineers were shot for their advice, and the project began. It was to be a great prestige project for Rumanian Communism. 200,000 political prisoners and criminals toiled to build the Canal, working in winter in temperatures of minus 25°C and during the summer in heat like an oven. Living in ram- shackle barracks, behind barbed wire, the slave labourers had to shovel earth into barrows under the blows of the guards. Workers died every day from exhaustion and hunger.

Richard was horrified. It was worse than the slavery of the Israelites under Pharaoh. He would have been even more horrified had he known that his own beloved Sabina was a slave there. The Secret Police had come for her in the middle of the night of August 22nd, 1950. Fortunately, she had sent Mihai away from the heat of Bucharest to have a holiday with some family friends in the north. When he returned, she was gone. Six months later — it was January 6th, Mihai's birthday — she had left Jilava where she was being held and started on the weary journey by prison train to Cernavoda on the Danube. From there the new batch of slaves were marched to the Canal.

Sabina suffered dreadfully. Being tiny, she was a particular butt of the guards who would toss her into the icy water for sport and then fish her out again to shiver in her wet clothes for the rest of the day. She ate grass and snakes and rats and dogs to keep herself alive. If Richard had known of her suffering, he might have broken down completely; mercifully, he did not know.

There were changes in the Government during 1952. The three leaders who had ruled Rumania since the Communist takeover were 'purged', including the hated Ana Pauker. It made no difference at Tirgul-Ocna. Prisoners came and went, men suffered and died just the same. It was a bitter winter and the half-starved prisoners coughed and shivered beneath their thin blankets.

In February 1953 something wonderful happened.

A prisoner called Avram Radonovici was brought into Room 4 to die. He was another 'intellectual', a former music critic from Bucharest. He was desperately ill with T.B. and because it had affected his spine, he was encased in plaster of Paris from chest to thighs. The other prisoners watched in amazement from their beds as he put his hand into the top of the dirty plaster cast and extracted a small, tattered book.

A book! Richard had not seen one since 1948!

'Would you like to borrow it?' Avram asked. Richard received it reverently; it was a copy of St. John's Gospel.

The book went from hand to hand round the ward.

Everybody read it, savoured it, discussed it, learned passages by heart. To Richard the book was a special blessing for it distressed him that he was beginning to forget so many passages of the Bible which had once been dear and familiar to him. As he read again the beautiful words, he was reminded how their truth was demonstrated every day of his imprisonment. 'The Comforter', as Jesus promised, was with him all the time, calming his anxiety, enabling him to bear the pain of his illness, giving him the strength not to surrender.

In March of 1953, Stalin died. When the news reached Tirgul-Ocna prison, hopes ran high that conditions might improve. An official high up in the prison department inspected their quarters and asked if they had any complaints. Most of the prisoners feared it was a trick and kept silent but Richard spoke what was in all their hearts to say:

'Can you not see that we are victims of injustice? Perhaps in the Party's eyes we are guilty men but we were sentenced to prison, not a long-drawn-out death sentence. Look at our food, our lack of heating and medicine, look at the dirt and the disease. Ask about the barbarities men have endured. In God's name, do not wash your hands of us as Pilate did of Christ.'

Encouraged by Richard's outspokenness, some of the others ventured to speak. The Inspector looked and listened and went away to make his report. A week later, the prison commandant was dismissed. After that, conditions at Tirgul-Ocna improved. With better food, Richard became slightly stronger and, for the first time in two years, was able to sit out of bed and even begin to walk a little. Dr. Aldea brought another doctor to see him and they examined him thoroughly.

'We can't make you out,' said Dr. Aldea. 'Your lungs are like a sieve, your spine is affected. You have had no drugs or medical attention. You're no better than when I saw you first two years ago — but you are certainly no worse. I think we will move you back to the general ward.'

Richard was the first man ever to leave Room 4 alive.

CHAPTER 10

An Unexpected Reprieve

IN 1955, RUMANIA was admitted to the United Nations. It horrified those in prison that, despite the U.N. Charter binding members to political and religious freedom, they were still kept confined. At least, however, there were changes for the better.

Gheorgiu-Dej was now dictator of Rumania. He admitted that grave mistakes had been made by the previous administration and promised to put them right. One of the worst mistakes had been the Danube–Black Sea Canal. It had cost millions of *lei* and thousands of lives, yet after nearly four years only five of its projected forty miles were completed. The project was abandoned.

While the prison discussed this news, one of Richard's friends took him on one side and told him that Sabina had been at the Canal. He had not dared tell Richard until he was strong enough to take the news and now, piecing together scraps of information gleaned from new prisoners, he was able to assure Richard that his wife was alive, though in hospital.

Richard was shattered by the news. For the first time in years, he was unable to pray. Sabina in *that* place! How many years had she been away from home? Where was Mihai? But there was no answer to these questions.

For a while under the new dictatorship, each prisoner was allowed one monthly parcel. With what expectation they were opened and the food and cigarettes shared round! The prisoners were allowed to state their requirements on a post-card — this, in itself, a wonderful concession for up to now they had not been allowed to write home at all — but the items they could ask for were limited. Richard's card was setting a problem for his friends in Bucharest. He asked for 'Dr. Filon's old clothes'. Dr. Filon was a small man, Richard was six feet two. How could the doctor's clothes possibly fit him? But it must mean something. At last they found a solution. The 'old clothes' were only an excuse to mention a doctor, and Tirgul-Ocna was known to be a prison specially for prisoners suffering from T.B. They knew that Richard himself had had the disease. The cryptic message must mean that he was asking for any drugs that could be spared. The Americans had discovered streptomycin ten years before and it was producing wonderful results among T.B. sufferers. When it was first announced, the discovery had been dismissed as Western propaganda but now, ten years later, the drug's value was acknowledged. Richard's friends sent him 100 grammes of streptomycin — which he promptly gave to the inmates of Room 4.

Where some prisoners rejoiced only in the receipt of their parcels, Richard had the added joy of knowing that his parcel would be blessed with the prayers of all his friends. They would know now for certain that he was still alive, that their prayers for his safety had been heard.

A letter — the first over all the long years of his imprisonment — arrived for Richard from Sabina. It contained three sentences, all she was allowed to write, but it filled him with joy. 'She was well. She was still confined to Bucharest. Mihai would be coming to see him soon.' Mihai coming to see him! Richard had left him when he was nine. Now he was sixteen!

He was separated from his son by the length of the room. Only a small grating allowed him to see the thin lanky youth who answered to the summons of 'Mihai Wurmbrand'. All Mihai could see on the other side of the grating was a shaven head, a gaunt, grey face with enormous eyes and a white stubble on the chin. But the smile had the sweetness he remembered. The boy's words came with a rush, in case he was interrupted by the guards: 'Mother's well. She couldn't come. She says to tell you that even if you die in prison, you must not be sad because we'll all meet in heaven.'

That told Richard much. He had worried in case Mihai had lost his faith.

'Have you food at home?'

'Yes, our Father is very rich. He provides.'

The guards sniggered. They assumed Mihai meant his mother had divorced Richard (as happened in many cases to long-term prisoners) and had married again, but Richard knew what Mihai meant.

But what could father and son do with a few minutes after a separation of seven years? The last time they spoke together, Mihai was a child; now he was a young man. They could not even reach out a hand to each other. Both were so overcome with emotion that they could find no words to say.

The new leniency did not last long. The old restrictions were restored, new ones devised — even petty tyrannies like closing up the windows in the wards and painting them over so that the prisoners had no fresh air and could not see the sky. Richard's illness flared up again. In June, he learned he was to be transferred to another prison. Dr. Aldea was worried.

'You're not fit to move but there's nothing I can do about it. But if you receive any more streptomycin, *don't give it away!*'

The prisoners who were being transferred had to lie on the ground in the prison yard while the blacksmith chained their ankles for the journey. One of the officers who knew Richard's stubborn courage stood over him and mocked:

'Surely *you* have something to say about being put in irons?'

Richard replied from where he lay on the ground 'Yes, lieutenant. I'd like to sing you a little song', and he broke into the opening words of the Rumanian Republic's new national anthem: 'Broken chains are left behind us . . .' Fortunately for Richard, the transport arrived before the officer had recovered from his shock.

This time Richard went to Craiova prison in southern Rumania. Like Japanese porters packing commuter trains at rush hour, the guards pushed the new prisoners into cells already crowded. Bunks rose in tiers, each bunk containing at least two men. More men squatted half-naked on the floor or leaned against the walls. It was like a scene out of hell. Richard spent two months there. It was noisy, insanitary and squalid and these conditions made the prisoners hostile to any attempt Richard made to preach the gospel. But all prisoners long for the same thing: relief from boredom. So Richard turned his sermons into thrillers. The prisoners hung on his words, though one of them said: 'Pastor, I've heard many crime stories, but none like yours, which always end with the criminal, the victim and the policeman all going to church together.' He could have told stories for twenty-four hours a day and still he would not have satisfied the demand. He told them the life stories of well-known gangsters and criminals and showed how lack of love had turned them to evil ways; he broke up long novels he had read many years before into serials: Dostoievsky's *Crime and Punishment*, Tolstoy's *Resurrection*, Hamsun's *Hunger*. The last of these brought tears to many eyes for the food in Craiova prison was the worst that any of them had encountered — and most of them had had years of experience of prison food.

One day, however, the guards brought in a huge canister of onion soup, another of stew with real meat in sizeable pieces. There were mounds of carrots and creamy white potatoes, two bread rolls for each prisoner, a basket of fresh apples. What could it mean? Had the American Army taken over Rumania? They savoured every mouthful. An hour later, one of the prisoners called excitedly from the window: 'Women! Look — there are women!' The rest crowded to

look out. 'Oh, dammit, they're leaving.' Down below by the
prison gate they could see the Commandant saying good-bye
to a party of well-dressed ladies. 'A delegation from the
West,' a guard told them later. 'They thought the prison diet
was excellent,' he added maliciously.

The next day, the prisoners were back on rotten tripe and
cabbage.

During the next few months, Richard moved round several different prisons. The journeys followed the same grim
pattern: the closed, crowded railway trucks; the shackles
that rubbed sores on his ankles that took months to heal. He
spent a short time at Poarta-Alba where Sabina had worked
in the forced-labour camp. The Canal project had been
abandoned and the old barrack huts where the slave labourers had been housed were now derelict. Even so, they made
Richard feel very close to Sabina.

At his next prison, Gherla, Richard was allowed a brief
visit from his wife. They were separated from each other by
the length of the room, shouting distance away from each
other. An officer and guards looked on. Sabina looked so
tiny. Her hair was still dark, though streaked with grey. Her
face was lined but smiling, and filled with a peace and
beauty Richard had never seen before.

'Are you all right at home?'

'Yes, we are all well. Praise be to God.'

'*You are not allowed to mention God,*' interrupted the
officer.

'Is my mother still alive?'

'Praise God, she is still alive.'

'*You are not allowed to mention God here!*'

Sabina asked: 'How are *you*?'

'I'm in the prison hospital . . .'

'*You are not allowed to say where you are in prison.*'

'About my trial — is there any hope of appeal?'

'*You are not allowed to discuss your trial.*'

Everything they tried to say to each other was blocked in

this way. Eventually Richard said: 'Go home, Sabina dear. They won't let us speak.'

His tuberculosis worsened. He was sent back to the prison hospital at Vacaresti where he had spent the month immediately prior to his trial. Two officers who arrived to interrogate him asked him what he thought of Communism now.

'I really cannot say,' was his reply. 'I only know it from the inside of prisons.'

From Vacaresti hospital to Jilava prison — the worst of any Richard experienced. The name means 'wet place' in Rumanian and it was aptly named. The prison was largely underground, a warren of corridors and ill-lit cells where water dripped constantly from the roof and trickled down the walls. There was no spark of community spirit at Jilava. It was a transit jail where men often met old enemies who had denounced them and who were now denounced themselves. Here Richard met a familiar figure, Colonel Dulgheru. He was no longer arch-inquisitor of the Secret Police but a prisoner himself, and terrified lest any of his former victims should recognise him.

On a June day in 1956, Richard's name was called.

'Interrogation at once. Move!'

He rose to his feet wearily. The thought of more bullying questions was almost more than he could bear.

'Come on! Come on! They're waiting!'

But there was no interrogator waiting. Outside the cell there was only an official who thrust a piece of paper into Richard's hands. It was a court order stating that under an amnesty his prison sentence had been suspended. He was free! He could not grasp the significance of what it said.

'But I've only done eight of my twenty years . . .'

'Get going.'

'But look at me. I'll be arrested by the first policeman I meet . . .'

'We've no spare clothes here. Move!'

The gate clanged shut behind him.

Jilava is three miles from Bucharest. Richard shuffled down the white dusty road in his broken shoes and tattered prison garments. The air was full of the sounds and scents of summer.

'Dear God!' he said out loud. 'Help me not to rejoice more because I am free than because You were with me in prison!'

An old peasant and his wife came towards him. 'You come from *there*?' they asked, eyeing his scarecrow appearance. The man pulled out a *leu*, the smallest Rumanian coin, and pressed it into Richard's hand.

A little farther, another woman stopped him. 'You come from *there*?' He nodded. They sat down on a wall together in the sunshine and she asked if he had news of the priest of her village, arrested some months before. She, too, pressed a coin into his hand. 'For the tram fare,' she said.

People crowded round him at the tram stop. He was easy to recognise as a released prisoner and all wanted to know if he had seen their husband, their father, their brother, their son. It seemed as if every family in Rumania had somebody in prison. As the tram moved off from the terminus in the direction of Bucharest, a policeman on a motor bike roared up and yelled to the driver. Richard's heart almost stopped. Surely they could not be coming to take him back! But it was only to report that a passenger had boarded the tram after the doors were shut and was still clinging to the outside step.

The woman next to Richard on the tram had a basket of strawberries on her knee.

'Have you had any this year?' she asked.

'Not for eight years!'

She told him to eat his fill and he crammed his mouth with the sweet fruit as the tram carried him into the familiar streets of Bucharest.

When he opened the front door of his home, there were a number of strange young people in the hall. They looked at him curiously. He was filthy and in rags, but Mihai recognised him.

'Father!'

Sabina came and Richard's eyes blurred with tears as he held her in his arms.

There was still not to be any peace. People had recognised him on the way home and had been telephoning all over Bucharest. The door-bell rang continually with visitors and Richard had to stand in the hall in his patched prison trousers tied up with string and accept the greetings of his flock. Their Pastor had returned.

It was late that night before they were alone together. Richard lay beside Sabina in the strangely clean bed. He could not sleep. He went across to Mihai's room and looked down at his sleeping son. So often in prison he had dreamed he was at home, only to wake to the emptiness of his cell. But Mihai was there, and Sabina was there. And God was there. He had come home.

CHAPTER 11

Back to Prison

RICHARD SPENT TWO weeks in hospital and then he returned to the work of the Underground Church. The Mission was still closed and he no longer had his job with the World Council of Churches, so he and Sabina were very poor. But at least they had a roof over their heads — quite literally so, as they were now three people occupying the two small attic rooms that had been allotted to Sabina and Mihai.

During Richard's imprisonment, Sabina had been unable to obtain regular work and things would have gone hard for her had it not been for their friends and for Mihai. The boy had gone to work at the age of eleven for it was difficult to find a school that would keep him. Whenever it was discovered that he was the son of a political prisoner, he was expelled. He managed to secure a job as assistant to the piano tuner at the Opera House and with the small wage he earned, he and Sabina had been able to survive. He had continued his education at evening classes.

Richard could not rest. During his eight years in prison, he had seen Communism at its most evil yet had seen how the love of God could transmute that evil into a kind of peace. 'Do not fear the Cross! You will find it the greatest of joys!' He began to explain this to Sabina but found it did not need explaining. She also had borne her cross in triumph among the horrors of the slave camp and had come through with a serenity that matched Richard's own. Now Richard felt he must take that message of love to as many as would hear it, and use that love to fight the evil of Communism.

He accepted an invitation to give a series of lectures at the

University in the ancient town of Cluj. A zealous 'informer' reported to the authorities that the lectures were to take place and an official from the Ministry of Cults, a fanatical Communist called Rugojanu, was sent to report what sedition Richard preached.

On the first evening, about fifty students and a few tutors attended. Richard recognised Rugojanu at once as a spy. The first lecture was to be on the theory of evolution.

'Was it not strange,' Richard began, 'that the new Rumania, so advanced and Socialist, rejected all capitalist ideas except the one put forward by the English bourgeois, Charles Darwin?'

It was a brilliant lecture. On the surface, everything Richard said was entirely in accordance with the Party line but everyone in the audience, including Rugojanu, knew that Richard was preaching the Good News of Jesus.

The following evening, the audience had doubled, and by the end of the week, the lecture hall was packed with over a thousand students and lecturers. The atmosphere was charged with expectation, like the time of Richard's defiant speech at the Congress of Cults when the Communists first came to power.

'Remember that there is always hope,' he concluded. 'The wheel of life keeps turning. It put me in prison; now I am free. I have been ill; now I am better . . .'

'Sedition! Sedition!' shouted Rugojanu. 'The wheel will not turn. Communism is here for ever!'

'But I didn't mention Communism,' said Richard. 'I merely said the wheel of *life* keeps turning . . .'

'But you meant it. Don't think you've heard the last of this. I'll see you never preach again.' He did not interrupt any more that day for he could see the enthusiasm with which Richard's words were received, but the next day at the Conference of Pastors he attacked Richard again. He worked himself into a passion of anger and rushed out crying 'Wurmbrand is finished! Wurmbrand is finished!'

He flung out of the building in his rage. A car, swerving to miss a dog in the road, skidded, mounted the pavement and crushed Rugojanu against the wall. He died instantly.

Richard no longer had a licence to preach but that did not stop him. He worked with a sense of urgency for he knew he had not long. He held his services in attics and basements, in open fields and once, even, in the home of a high-ranking official in the Secret Police who was on holiday and whose maid was a secret Christian. But there was always danger, not least from former prison friends turned informers who begged for help 'for old time's sake' in the desperate hope of picking up information they could sell in exchange for bread.

After the crushing of revolt in Hungary by the Russians in 1956 attacks on so-called 'superstition' in Rumania became even more violent. Churches were closed and turned into Communist clubs or cinemas or warehouses. Yet more ministers and priests were rounded up and thrown into prison.

Richard prayed: 'Lord, if there are any in prison that I can help, send me back there and I will bear it willingly.'

They came for him at one o'clock in the morning of January 15th, 1959.

This time both Sabina and Mihai were present at his 'trial'. It was a repeat of the secret proceedings that had been held in Vacaresti prison hospital so many years before. Once again the proceedings took ten minutes. Richard's suspended sentence was restored and increased from twenty years to twenty-five.

After a few days in Jilava prison just outside Bucharest Richard was taken to Gherla in Transylvania where he and Sabina had had that brief meeting three years before. The prison was terribly overcrowded, 10,000 prisoners being herded into accommodation intended for 2,000. Once again, Richard had to share a bunk in one of the gloomy barrack-like cells. Discipline was harsh. Prisoners were flogged — twenty-five lashes — for the slightest offence.

Everyone committed at least one 'offence' during his stay. Richard and a high-ranking member of the Orthodox Church were assigned, among other jobs, the unpleasant task of emptying the slops for the hundred men in their cell.

There were not only priests and intellectuals there but murderers, thieves and war criminals. They were bitter, angry men and some of them saw a chance to work out their frustrations by beating up Richard because he was a Jew. A warder broke up one such scuffle but in the poor light could not recognise who was involved.

'Who did this?' he demanded of Richard.

'I can't say. As a Christian, I love my enemies. I don't denounce them.'

So Richard was flogged for insolence — but at least he earned the respect of his fellow-prisoners, even though they did not understand him.

They did not understand him, either, when he refused to taunt an ex-soldier for executing Jews during the war.

'Can't you understand that that was twenty years ago?' Richard begged. 'He has paid for his crime with years of hunger and beatings in prison. He's grown up since then. Would you call a man illiterate all his life because he couldn't read at the age of three?'

Once again, as at Tirgul-Ocna, the prisoners kept up their spirits with riddles and jokes.

'A man travelling on a train has a wife called Eve and they live in a red house. What's his name?' asked Gaston, a Unitarian pastor. 'Can't you guess it? His name is Charles.'

'But why? We can't work it out.'

'Easy! I've known him for years.'

Archimandrite Miron (who shared Richard's job of 'slopping out') told what he swore was a true story: A prison commandant was inspecting a batch of new prisoners.

'What is your crime?' he asked one man.

'I've done nothing, sir, and I've got ten years.'

'And what is *your* crime?' the commandant asked the next prisoner.

'Nothing, sir, and I've got twenty years.'

'Lying swine!' shouted the commandant. 'Nobody in the People's Republic gets more than ten years for doing nothing!'

Richard was shocked one day to meet again among a group of new prisoners Professor Popp whom he had known at Tirgul-Ocna. Popp was one of the prisoners there who had displayed great goodness and a strong Christian faith. They had both been released during the 1956 amnesty but had not seen each other since. Now Professor Popp looked old, ill and depressed. He told Richard the reason why.

On his release from prison, he had gone mad for pleasure. He felt that time had passed him by; he wanted to make up for the lost years so he spent every penny he had on pleasure; he drank too much; he left his wife for a much younger woman. Inevitably, for he was basically a good man, he felt remorse for his foolishness.

'I wanted to come and talk to you,' he told Richard 'but I lived miles from Bucharest. So I went to a local pastor and confessed everything to him. I told him that if it hadn't been for Communism, I'd never have been in prison in the first place so really Communism was to blame for my troubles. The pastor listened — and denounced me.'

Popp had been sentenced to another twelve years for speaking against Communism but he seemed as if he could no longer cope with imprisonment. One day soon after this conversation, his control snapped and he attacked the room leader like a madman. He was dragged off to the prison hospital where he died the following day.

Inevitably, after this tragedy, there was much discussion of life after death, even among the hardened criminals. A man called Florescu, a professional thief, declared:

'I believe in what I can see, taste and feel. We're all

matter, like this wooden stool I'm sitting on. When you're dead, that's it.'

Richard kicked the stool from under him and Florescu fell backwards to the floor. He scrambled to his feet and went for Richard. 'What's the idea?' he demanded.

'But you said you were matter, just like the stool,' reasoned Richard. 'I didn't hear the stool complain!'

Everybody laughed — even Florescu — and Richard went on to develop his point that man has a spirit that makes him different from inanimate objects. Everyone hung on his words. When a man is in prison, with little expectation of release, the idea of survival *after* death brings a message of hope.

Pastor Gaston alone seemed unable to derive any comfort from Richard's words.

'What is on your mind?' Richard asked him. 'You are fretting over something. Why don't you take your problem to Jesus. He will give you comfort and strength.'

Gaston sighed. 'You make it sound as if He was here with us, alive.'

'Certainly he's alive,' Richard replied. 'I'll prove it to you.'

Gaston shook his head sadly. 'How you persist!' he said. 'You're worse than a Communist!'

Shortly afterwards, Gaston was moved to a different cell. They did not see each other again for several months and then in bitter circumstances. Richard had been flogged yet again on some trivial pretext. He was flung into the isolation cell afterwards and found Gaston there in a dreadful state. His back was a mass of bloody wounds and he was weak and feverish. But despite his suffering, he insisted that he must confess a big sin to Richard — the sin that had been preying on his mind for months. He, Gaston, had been the pastor who had denounced Professor Popp!

'I was weak,' he sobbed. 'I couldn't stand it when they

threatened me. But when I saw him here . . . and then when he died! I can never forgive myself!'

Richard tried to comfort him. He told him how all Sabina's family had died in a pogrom but how, when she met one of the men who carried out the slaughter, she forgave him and helped him to become a Christian and how, thereafter, the man's whole life was changed.

'Popp would have forgiven you, too,' Richard assured Gaston. 'Particularly if he had known the pressures being applied to you.'

But here was yet another tragedy of the Communist system that caused a man to turn against his brother in the faith, one member of a family to inform against the rest. At least prison only made brutes of some; it made saints of others.

Apart from an occasional change of population, there was no relief at Gherla from the monotonous round of hardship, cruelty and degradation. Month succeeded month, year succeeded tedious year. Sometimes it seemed that time and life itself were standing still, like the clock over the prison gates that had been stopped ever since anyone could remember.

CHAPTER 12

On The Brink

IN MARCH 1962 a new Commandant came to the prison at Gherla. One of his first actions was to segregate prisoners according to their former occupations rather than having them all mixed up together. Richard should have been placed in the cell with priests and clergy but because he insisted that he was a 'pastor' he was grouped with agricultural workers — 'pastor' in Rumanian means 'shepherd'. However, the error was soon discovered and, after the usual beating, Richard was moved into a cell with a hundred other clergy.

This should have been the most peaceful and united cell in the whole prison but such was not the case. Just as at the time of his conversion, Richard had found it difficult to find a denomination that seemed to him truly *Christian*, so now he found that even Christian priests who were prepared to suffer nobly in prison for their faith could not agree together. Instead of having one united act of worship that would witness for Christ before the Communist guards, they squabbled over different forms of the Mass, over whether the Virgin Mary was 'Queen of Heaven' or merely 'Patron of Hungary', and such-like questions of dogma. There were scarcely two men of different sects who would say together the Family Prayer, 'Our Father'. It was a tragic situation. Time and again, Richard insisted:

'What matters is respect for the Scriptures as the only rule, and salvation by faith in Jesus. The names and forms don't count.'

The Commandant's purpose was succeeding most notably. By shutting up all the priests and clergy together, not only did he deprive the other prisoners of any form of spiritual comfort, he was also leaving the different priests to destroy each other. Thus began for Richard what was to be the very worst period of his whole long imprisonment.

It began with a series of 'indoctrination' lectures, often ridiculous in themselves but all part of a clever long-term plan.

The ridiculous side was apparent in the very first lecture which was given by an earnest young political officer. It concerned the eclipse of the sun that would shortly be taking place. He explained the nature of the solar system and announced that since it was the desire of the People's Republic of Rumania to broaden the views of the people, the prisoners were to be allowed to watch the eclipse from the courtyard.

Up went someone's hand. 'Please, if it rains, can we have the eclipse indoors?'

'No!' replied the lecturer seriously, and went on with his discourse.

The long-term strategy of the lectures was very clever. As the weeks went by, the subjects of the lectures changed subtly. From general information, they turned to politics, from politics to atheism. All the time there were included in the lectures reminders of what the prisoners were missing in the world outside: food, drink, entertainment, sex. It stirred up feelings and desires long kept under control. Men became restless and frustrated. At first, the audiences at the lectures were encouraged to ask questions — an opportunity Richard seized on every possible occasion. With his quick brain, he could usually run rings round the lecturer and show up the weakness of his argument. If he was too impertinent in his comments, Richard would be slapped around the face — but that seemed a small price to pay for witnessing to his beliefs. But it was all very puzzling. When years of torture, insult and starvation had not weakened his Christian beliefs, how could a few lectures make any difference? Richard had not anticipated how sophisticated the Communists had become in their methods of indoctrination.

Loud speakers had been installed all over the prison soon after the new Commandant's arrival. Now, as the lectures got under way, they crackled into life:

> 'Communism is good.
> Communism is good.
> Communism is good.'

It went on for hours and hours so that, even when the tape had been switched off, the words 'Communism is good' continued to ring in everyone's ears. It was the beginning of a technique of 'brain-washing' which Russian and Chinese Communists have brought to perfection.

As the broadcasts continued, so the lectures continued — now with more emphasis on worldly things.

'So much pleasure waits for you outside,' the lecturer would say. 'And *you* can enjoy it, if only you will be sensible. Throw away the outworn ideas you have had for so long and come over to our side.'

Prison food, hitherto so scanty as to keep men hopeless and apathetic, was now slightly improved so that all aspects of men's appetites revived and deprivation became the more cruel to bear. Richard suspected also that the food was drugged.

'You've only one life,' the lecturer said each day. 'It passes so quickly. We want to help you to make the most of it. Why waste it in prison? Why not throw in your lot with us?'

In between the lectures, the tape-recorders continued their insidious message: 'Communism is good! Communism is good!'

Many prisoners gave way under the strain — good men who had withstood as much as fifteen years of imprisonment and torture weakened under this persistent attack on their senses.

'I have been a fool . . .' they would cry. 'I have been misled by Capitalist and Christian lies ... Never again will I set foot in a Church ... Let me embrace Communism and live!'

Though many in the 'priests' room' did recant in this way, the remainder became more closely-knit in loyalty to their faith. Old divisions were set aside and the cell became ablaze with renewed faith. They all knew that their stubbornness would inevitably lead to further suffering but it seemed at times, Richard said, as if there were angels all around them.

One Sunday morning, all the occupants of the prison were ordered into the yard to watch an hour-long play. The action mocked Christianity, and the Commandant and his officers laughed and clapped. Every time this happened, the prisoners were ordered to laugh and clap as well, and when the play was over each prisoner in turn had to go to the front of the audience and make comments on the play. It was not just enough to say that he had enjoyed it; he had to give reasons. One after another went up to the front and repeated some slogan against religion. It was not worth another beating to be defiant. How much easier just to say what was required and maybe not be noticed for a few hours.

This was the problem that faced Richard when his turn came. He walked slowly to the front, conscious that every eye was upon him. He was well-known at Gherla. His name had become a by-word for courage throughout the prison population of Rumania; and many of the priests in the yard that morning had been at the Congress of Cults in 1945 when Richard had spoken so powerfully for his Lord and Saviour. Would *he* praise Communism now?

'Go on, speak!' ordered the Commandant. If he could only break the stubborn ones like Wurmbrand, the rest would be easy.

Richard thought for a moment. What should he say? Then he remembered Sabina's words, all those years before: 'Wash this shame from the face of Christ!'

He began: 'It is Sunday morning. At home, our wives and mothers and children are praying for us at church or in their homes. We should have liked to have been praying for them but, instead, we have had to watch this play.'

There was absolute silence in the prison yard. He continued:

'Many of you here have spoken against Jesus, but what have you against Him? You speak of the proletariat, but wasn't Jesus a carpenter? You denounce wealth, but didn't Jesus drive the moneylenders with whips from the Temple?'

There was much more in this vein, with quotations from Communism's own authors backing up Richard's case for Christ. The Commandant shifted uncomfortably in his chair but did not interrupt. Moved by the intensity of the listening, Richard forgot that he was in prison. He was no longer cautious in what he said but openly preached Christ, what He had done for mankind, what He should mean to every man present.

'What is more,' Richard concluded. 'Just as every schoolboy is examined at the year's end, just as every factory hand has his work scrutinised by the overseer, just so will every life be judged by God!'

He turned and pointed an accusing finger at the Commandant. 'You will be judged too, Major,' he said.

The prisoners broke into cheers but Richard knew it was only a tiny victory. He would have to pay for it. The next day he was told two things: that his wife was in prison and that he was to be flogged that evening for his insolence at the play.

All the time he was waiting for the flogging, Richard was worrying about Sabina. Her health had not been good since her ordeal at the Canal. Where would she be sent this time?

The hours dragged by. Someone in the next room was beaten. Richard could hear the blows falling and the screams of pain, but nobody came for him that night . . . or the next night . . . or the one after. For six days, he was warned each morning to expect his punishment before nightfall so that he spent six days in tense expectation of the ordeal to come. On the sixth night he was flogged, brutally, then flung back into his cell where the loudspeakers were blaring:

> 'Christianity is stupid.
> Why not give it up?
> Christianity is stupid.
> Why not give it up?'

The beatings, the mocking, the brainwashing continued. Some men gave way; others continued to hold fast. One day Richard was taken out of the 'priests' cell' and thrust, alone and handcuffed, into a white-tiled room. It was brilliantly lit and terribly hot. Loudspeakers kept up the insistent message:

> 'Nobody believes in Christ now.
> No-one goes to Church.
> Give it up.
> Give it up.
> Nobody believes in Christ now . . .'

Hour followed hour. Sweat soaked his body and trickled into his eyes. The white tiles glared in the electric light.

> 'Nobody believes in Christ now.
> Give it up . . . Give it up . . . Give it up . . .'

He wanted to put his fingers in his ears to blot out the insidious voice but he could not for his wrists were tied.

'*I* believe in God,' he shouted back at the loudspeakers. '*I* won't give it up. *I* won't give it up. *I believe!*'

The cell became hotter as the heating was turned up.

'Nobody believes in Christ now.
Give it up . . . Give it up . . . Give it up . . .'

Richard began to say the Lord's Prayer. 'Our Father, who art in Heaven . . .' What came next? 'Our Father . . . Our Father . . .' Surely there was more to it than that but *he could not remember the words*. 'Jesus! Jesus!' he murmured. Over and over again. 'Jesus! Jesus!'

He closed his eyes against the brightness and tried to turn his thoughts inwards, away from the insistent message of atheism. The Communists must be very afraid of God if they were prepared to go to such lengths to defeat Him. That thought comforted him and he became quieter, husbanding his resources, for he did not know how many hours he would have to endure this torture.

'Jesus lives,' he repeated to himself over and over again. 'He lives. He lives.'

After a while he found his own thoughts were sounding louder to him than the voices of the loudspeakers and he knew that Jesus was with him in the cell, comforting and sustaining him. He was even able to pray for the Commandant who had decreed this treatment.

'Father, forgive them for they know not what they do.' Jesus's words held a new depth of meaning. Could he blame the Commandant for being ruthless if no-one had ever shown him any other way of behaving? Richard lay on the floor of the stifling, brilliantly-lit room and prayed for his torturers.

The next morning, half-fainting from heat and lack of sleep, he was led into another room and left alone. The room was blessedly cool and fresh. There was a bed in one corner with smooth, clean sheets; a change of clothes laid out on a chair; a table with flowers. Richard sat down on the chair and wept. Comfort after so much suffering was just too much to bear. When he had recovered his composure a little, he noticed that there was a folded newspaper on the table — the first he had seen since January 1959. It was now July 1963!

The Commandant came in. What did Richard think of his room, he asked. Was it not pleasant — an example of the comfort he could enjoy under Communism if he would only deny this foolish God of his, admit that it was all superstition. Richard pulled himself together with an effort. He must not show weakness now. He picked up the newspaper and pointed to the date.

'If there is no Christ,' he asked, 'how is it that you date your paper 1,963 years after the birth of someone who never existed?'

He passed the next few weeks between the restful room with the flowers and the white-tiled cell with the loudspeakers and the blinding lights. On August 23rd, the day on which Rumania celebrated the foundation of the People's Republic, he was taken down to watch the television news programme showing the celebrations and parades. He was profoundly shaken by what he saw. There were bands and processions, banners, crowds shouting 'August 23rd brings us freedom!' Was this real — surely it was largely mass hysteria? When he was asked to give his opinion of the Freedom Day Celebrations, he replied stubbornly:

'August 23rd freed our country from Fascism, but I was free long before that. Jesus set me free from sin and death.'

'Tell that nonsense to Yuri Gagarin,' laughed the Commandant. 'He has been up in space and he saw no sign of your God.'

'If an ant walked round the sole of my shoe,' Richard retorted. 'It could say it saw no sign of Wurmbrand.'

More time in the punishment cell. 1963 moved into 1964.

Early that year, Richard was visited by a delegation of high-ranking officials led by Negrea, the Deputy Minister for the Interior. They had been studying Richard's case, they told him, and although they did not agree with his views, they respected his stubborn integrity. They felt the time had come to settle differences. They would meet him half way. They would forget what he had done against the State. After all, they could use a man of his calibre ...

Richard was wary. Was this a new trap? Why should an important Minister come two hundred miles from Bucharest to Gherla just to see *him*? Negrea was confiding: 'We made a mistake, Mr. Wurmbrand, in attacking your World Council of Churches. You are widely known abroad and we still get enquiries about you. We're offering you the position of Lutheran Bishop-Elect of Rumania. The present Bishop is old; you would soon succeed him. All you have to do is co-operate with us, point out how we are all working together for peace and friendship. Just think what it would mean — a high salary, your family around you, comfort, freedom to preach ...'

It seemed a reasonable enough suggestion. After all, Richard thought, a lot of good could come out of such a compromise. He asked for time to think it over.

'Till Monday, then ...' Negrea shook hands courteously. 'I'll put your release papers through immediately.' He was very confident.

Richard returned to his cell and prayed. He said later that that weekend was for him his Gethsemane. *Must* he accept another eleven years in prison when he could be with Sabina and Mihai? Had he not suffered enough? But his heart answered him:

'You know what "co-operate" means: inform on your congregation, only preach what is acceptable to the Party. Do you want to be "Richard Wurmbrand, Lutheran Bishop of Rumania, *by appointment of the Secret Police*"?'

He knew he must say 'No' and for the first time for days felt tranquil in his soul.

He was kept on in the special block. The brainwashing continued:

> 'Christianity is dead . . .
> Christianity is dead . . .'

He was promised a visit from his family and sat all one long day in a clean shirt waiting for them to come, not knowing that there had been no visit arranged. He waited and waited. Nobody came.

'They don't want to know you any more . . .' said the loud-speakers. 'They don't want to know you any more . . .' Richard wept with disappointment.

So the months slid by.

> 'Christianity is dead . . .
> Christianity is dead . . .'

Almost, Richard began to believe the message of the loudspeakers. Almost . . . but not quite. A tiny spark of faith still flickered, despite fourteen years of imprisonment and torture, despite the past two dreadful years of brain-washing.

In June, all the prisoners were gathered together in the main hall of the prison. The Commandant addressed them. There had been a general amnesty. All 'political' prisoners were to be freed. It seemed unbelievable but it was true. There had been a slight 'thaw' in the relationship between the Communist countries and the West. Rumania's Prime Minister, Gheorgiu-Dej, was making a gesture towards greater liberality by releasing political prisoners.

Richard was one of the last hundred or so prisoners to be discharged. They stood around in the shabby but clean suits they had been given, waiting for their discharge papers.

'Brother Wurmbrand!' A voice hailed him. 'I'm so glad to have found you. I've heared so much about you from your son.'

The man introduced himself as coming from Sibiu. Richard turned to him eagerly.

'How is Mihai? What is he doing now?'

'He was well when I last saw him. We shared a cell together.'

'Mihai — in prison?' Richard was appalled.

'You mean you didn't know? He'd been inside for nearly six years.'

Nearly six years! That meant he must have been arrested almost at the same time as Richard.

The Commandant came up at that moment. 'Well, Wurmbrand. What will you do now that you are free?'

'I don't know.' For once, Richard was lost for words. 'I've nowhere to go. I was told officially some time ago that my wife had been arrested and now I find my son is in prison too. I don't know what I shall do.'

Richard had longed so much for this moment of release and now that it had arrived, the taste had turned bitter in his mouth. He walked out of Gherla prison into the bustle and colour of the little Transylvanian town. He had nothing except the second-hand suit he was wearing and a few *lei* in his pocket. He spent the money on a bus ticket to Cluj where he had given the defiant lectures at the University in 1957. The friends he had hoped to find there had moved. It was just one more disappointment heaped on top of the other. He tramped around the town, making enquiries, and at last found their new address. They were at home. What a welcome they gave him! How they pressed him to partake of cake and fruit, of all the best they had in their house! But the cake and the fruit could not compensate for the thought of the two empty attics that awaited him in Bucharest.

Richard asked if he could use his friends' telephone and

put through a call to his next-door neighbour in the capital.
The voice that answered was Sabina's!

'It's Richard,' he said. 'They told me you were in
prison.'

There was confusion at the other end of the line, then
Mihai's voice. 'Hold on. Mother's fainted.' A pause, then
'She's all right now. It was the shock. We'd been told you
were dead.'

So Mihai was not in prison either. Giving Richard false
news of his wife and son, giving Sabina false news of her
husband, had been just two last turns of the screw. What sort
of sadists were these people that they could so relish spoiling
a man's joy at his release?

There were crowds to welcome Richard when he arrived
at Bucharest station. The word had soon gone round and his
friends turned out with flowers to greet him. His head was
shaven, he was so emaciated he only weighed seven stone,
but the hollow eyes were as blue as ever. People packed into
their two attic rooms to talk to him, to shake him by the
hand.

The Pastor was back with his flock.

CHAPTER 13

Not Peace, But A Sword

RICHARD WURMBRAND spent several weeks in hospital after his release from prison. Despite his weakness and his need to build up his strength, people flocked to see him. He had become a legend in his own lifetime.

Even when he was barely strong enough, he resumed his work in the Underground Church, risking his liberty yet again in order to conduct secret services and to preach the Word of God to people long starved of spiritual food.

In vain the authorities tried to silence him. He was given a licence to preach and allotted an 'official' church at Orsova on the Yugoslavian border. The appointment was hedged round with restrictions and he was required to report on the people attending the services. He was instructed that his congregation could number 35 and no more; if 36 should ever attend, the church would be closed down. Richard refused to take the appointment. He would not turn informer. He knew that people were bound to flock to the church as soon as it was known that he was preaching there and he would not want to harm the little Christian community in Orsova by being the reason for its church's closure.

Prime Minister Gheorgiu-Dej died and the easier times following the amnesty came to an end. Restriction was piled on restriction, making church worship more and more difficult. Richard was in constant danger from the Secret Police; informers were everywhere.

He could not rest. Rumania had recently opened its doors to tourists from abroad and was visited also by delegations from the West. They were given specially prepared tours and programmes and went back to their home countries praising the great strides made by Rumania under the new Republic, expressing delight at the 'freedom of worship'. Little did they realise that the 'services' they attended had congregations of atheistic Party members 'packing the house'.

'You *must* go to the West,' Richard's friends urged him. 'Tell them the truth about our martyred Church. Be our voice in the free world. That must be your work from now on.'

It was not easy to 'go to the West'. It was not easy to leave Rumania at all — but there were ways. The country was short of foreign currency so it sold Jewish citizens for the sum of £1,000 per head. Richard, Sabina and Mihai put their names on the list. It took them a year to obtain permits to leave. Richard's 'price' was inflated to £2,500 but friends in the West loyally raised the money and at last they were free — though not without menaces.

'If you speak against our régime,' Richard was told, 'we can have you discredited, or kidnapped, or even killed.'

On December 6th, 1965 — the feast day in the Rumanian Orthodox Calendar of St. Nicholas, patron saint of prisoners — they flew from Bucharest to Rome. Right up to the moment of landing at Cimpino Airport, they still wondered whether something would happen to prevent their escape, whether the plane would turn back, whether they would be prevented from disembarking. But there was no hitch. They were indeed free.

Their visas were for Israel but the Jewish Welfare Agency, discovering they were Christian Jews, were not anxious to receive them. After frantic cabling and telephoning, they obtained fresh visas for Norway where friends of the Mission to Israel awaited them.

Everyone wanted to hear about their experiences. From Norway, they went to Britain, to America. Richard was called to testify before committees of the U.S. Senate and, later, of Congress. He made a moving plea for some, for *any* action to be taken that would help the thousands still being persecuted for their faith under Communism. 'One third of the world is entitled to one third of your prayers, of your concerns, of your gifts,' he said. He stripped off his shirt before the assembly and showed the marks of torture on his own body. At the same time as he urged prayers for Christians in Communist countries, Richard also warned of the danger of allowing Communism to spread.

'Don't think you only have a few Communists in your country,' he urged. 'That is what we thought in Rumania and look what happened. The free world is full not only of small but fervent official Communist parties but also of hidden Communists, waiting their opportunity to seize power. *They never give up.*'

He came to the West as a poor immigrant, possessing nothing except a vision — a vision that had been born and nurtured in prison cells, a vision of founding a Christian Mission to the Communist World. For this purpose, he feels, he was tested and tempered throughout fourteen years of imprisonment and torture; for this purpose his friends were enabled to buy his freedom.

Despite the threats that he was given before leaving Rumania, he felt compelled to write about his experiences. *Tortured for Christ* has been translated into twenty-five languages. He has made the world realise that the *least* a Christian can expect under Communism is the loss of his job or any chance of promotion; the worst is imprisonment, torture or even death, simply for the 'crime' of worshipping God. The policy of the Communist state is to make every citizen completely subservient to the system. Freedom of conscience, freedom of worship are forbidden.

In 1967, Richard began to circulate a monthly newsletter, *The Voice of the Martyrs*. Two thousand copies of the first issue were distributed in the United States. Now the newsletter is translated into thirty-three languages and is distributed in sixty-one countries. 'Read and pass it on' is printed in large letters on every copy, whether it be in Xhosa or Afrikaans, in English or Chinese. 'I cannot be silent until all have heard and respond', Richard writes. And people do respond, with their prayers, with their services, with their money. The new Mission grows and expands just as the missionary work of the early Church spread like wildfire round the world.

Christian Missions to the Communist World have been founded in forty-eight countries, from Iceland to India, from Australia to Peru, from the Cayman Islands to Canada. First and foremost, the Missions work to spread to Communist countries the Gospel, the Good News of Christ. They want the message to reach not only the 'Underground' Christians who are denied Bibles or other forms of Christian literature, but also the millions of people, particularly children, who are influenced by Communist doctrine only because they have never had a chance to hear anything else, who have been brain-washed from birth, who have never even heard the name of Christ.

The methods used by the Mission are varied and sometimes dangerous. Couriers smuggle literature under the very noses of Communist Customs officials. The early Christians risked their lives helping their imprisoned brethren; so do Christians today. Sometimes leaflets are dropped from planes. Balloons carrying a quarter of a million portions of the Gospels were released on one day when the prevailing wind would carry them into North Korea. Hundreds of thousands of Gospels are cast overboard in plastic bags where ocean currents will take them to the shores of Red China, Siberia, Albania, Cuba. Much goes astray, but enough gets through to make the expense and effort and risk worth while. Visitors to the free world from Communist countries — athletes, dancers, musicians, tourists, diplomats — are presented with 'free gifts' of Christian literature. During the Winter Olympic Games of 1968, a team from the Mission went to Grenoble and distributed Gospels among competitors from Communist countries. 'This is for old women,' objected one of the Russians. The girl who handed him the literature retorted 'Do *I* look like an old woman?' and that persuaded the Russian to accept the proffered Gospel.

With the same dual role of encouragement and conversion, broadcasts are relayed in fifty different languages to countries under Communist influence. Money is smuggled into Communist countries to enable secret Christians to buy radios to receive these programmes or to finance the setting up of secret printing presses to publish Bibles. Sometimes the money goes to support the families of Christians imprisoned or executed for their faith, or to pay the extortionate fines to which they are subjected.

The suffering of many of the underground Christians is almost unbelievable. In China in 1968, three teachers were publicly shot for teaching their class the Ten Commandments instead of Maoism. Reports reach the free world of the most cruel and sophisticated tortures being used to try to break the reason and spirit of Christians — yet still they maintain their faith and witness.

A Russian mother left with nine children to support after her husband had been thrown into prison for his faith was still able to write 'Glory be to the Lord that He has given us also a little chip of His cross to bear.' Families such as these need prayer support as well as food and clothing, so that another important aim of the Mission is to encourage prayer on behalf of the work — not only general prayer but praying for Christian martyrs by name. To this end, individual cases are described in the newsletters detailing the so-called 'crimes' of the persecuted Christians, together with their sentences.

Richard Wurmbrand devotes all his energies to furthering the work of the Missions. Through his books, articles, newsletters and personal contacts, he organises protests on behalf of persecuted Christians through Governments, Parliaments and Press. He exposes Communist infiltration into free societies. In particular, he works among young people in the free world who are vulnerable to the sinister and subversive propaganda of Communist agitators. It is work that calls for courage, but Richard has never lacked that quality. 'My manner of life is continual attack against the enemy,' he wrote, in April 1971, 'against openly manifested Communism, and against wolves in sheepskins, Communist tools disguised as pastors and priests ... Cowardice is cowardice even if you call it common sense, caution, circumspection. My doctrine knows none of these, but only one word: temerity.'

On October 22nd, 1967, a vast pro-Communist rally of some 60,000 persons marched to the Pentagon in Washington. Richard hired a truck with an extending crane (a cherry-picker') which lifted him above the heads of the protesters and kept pace with them as they marched. From this commanding position, he preached Christ to the marchers through a loud-hailer, and described some of the horrors Christians endured under Communism. Afterwards, many of the marchers crowded round him to hear more.

In March 1969, during a debate before students at San Fernando Valley College, U.SA., he had to struggle with his pro-Communist opponent to get hold of the microphone. In support of such action, he quotes John Wesley, that you are a real preacher only if, under your influence, some are converted and others get mad at you. Some people certainly 'get mad at' Richard Wurmbrand — but radical students accept Christ after such meetings, so the effort is worth while.

He is not without his critics. Much of this is because people are too credulous, too easily taken in by high-level assurances that there is freedom of worship under Communism. Richard knows otherwise, from experience. He is at times bitter in his denunciation of the apathy and com-

placency of the Church in the 'free world'. If only the
Church in the West had the passion of the Underground
Church — how it would be on fire for God! What could it
not achieve!

Other critics attack the Mission's work of smuggling
Bibles into Communist countries as immoral. Richard
replies: 'We consider rather as immoral to leave souls without the Word of God.' He justifies his methods by quoting
Paul's words in his first letter to the Corinthians, that he uses
'*all means*' to save men's souls.

But much of the criticism is due to the long arm of Communism reaching out, as threatened, to discredit his work.
He has been accused variously of being a C.I.A. agent, a
member of the Russian Secret Police, a Jesuit agent, a Zion-
ist, an anti-Semite, a Fascist, a murderer, even that he has
never lived in Rumania and has never been tortured! None
of this deters him. He analyses and ridicules each new accusation in his newsletters as fearlessly as he faces each new
challenge on a public platform.

In March 1972 he was addressing an assembly of 4,000 in
Basle, Switzerland. The platform was invaded by some
seventy or so members of a Left-Wing youth organisation
who seized the microphones and began singing revolutionary
songs, with clenched fists raised in the Communist salute.
Richard's words were drowned by the noise. The singing
continued despite protests from the audience, so Richard
clapped his hand over the leader's mouth to silence him.
Pandemonium broke out. Richard was attacked. Eventually the police arrived and used tear gas to break up
the mêlée. The very violence of the attacks against Richard
is an indication of the truth and importance of his
message.

He is in constant danger of assassination or kidnapping
but that does not deter him. He was due to preach in
Munich early in 1970 but was advised not to go as a plot to
murder him had been discovered. Richard went to Munich

notwithstanding. 'You never know,' he said. 'The one hired as a killer might be converted.' In India in 1972, he received a letter written in blood, threatening him with death if he preached. He still went into the pulpit in New Delhi and addressed a packed congregation. Whatever the threats, no matter how wearying the journeys, he still travels constantly all over the world — to Australasia, to Latin America, to Africa, to Europe — preaching, holding public meetings and debates, lobbying the most influential people in the countries he visits to join in the struggle against Communism. The very force of his personality sweeps aside any apathy and indifference in the people he meets.

He did not want to take on another struggle when he came out of prison. In his youth he had been dynamic, outgoing, eager to buttonhole the world with the message of Christ. Fourteen years in prison had changed that. The desire to convert men to Christ had not disappeared — that was as great as ever — but now he had become a more meditative man. So many years in solitary confinement had shown him the beauty of quietness. In 1965, he would have loved dearly to pass the remainder of his days peacefully with Sabina, in study and meditation and prayer. But, as his subsequent life has shown, it was not to be. Once again, he was to ask why 'as sons of peace, we do not bring peace, but a sword?' There is another story yet to be written of his life since 1965. The stage is wider than before but drama and danger are still as much part of the action.

As long as he has breath in his body, Richard will hate Communism — but he will still love the Communists, just as Jesus hated sin but loved the sinner. 'One must feed even those who curse God,' he has written. 'We must not be selective in our good deeds.'

Richard is in his middle sixties now. Despite his physical suffering, his hair is only streaked with grey and his tall figure walks erect, daring his enemies to do their worst. But his eyes have the tenderness and the glow of a man who has descended into hell and, with Christ at his side, has come back triumphant.

'A man *really* believes,' Richard once wrote, 'not what he recites in his creed, but only the things he is ready to die for.'

Such a man is Richard Wurmbrand.

Further Reading

SHOULD READERS wish *to learn more details of the events* described, they are recommended to read the books listed below. The author is sure they will be as much inspired and challenged by them as she was herself.

Books by Richard Wurmbrand:
    'Christ on the Jewish Road'
    'If Prison Walls Could Speak'
    'Sermons in Solitary Confinement'
    'If that were Christ, would you give Him your blanket?'
    'Tortured for Christ'
    'The Soviet Saints'
    'In God's Underground'
and by Sabina Wurmbrand:
    'The Pastor's Wife'
and by Michael Wurmbrand:
    'Christ or the Red Flag'

If you wish to receive *regular information* about *new books*, please send your name and address to:

London Bible Warehouse
PO Box 123
Basingstoke
Hants RG23 7NL

Name...

Address ....

....

....

....

I am especially interested in:
- ☐ Biographies
- ☐ Fiction
- ☐ Christian living
- ☐ Issue related books
- ☐ Academic books
- ☐ Bible study aids
- ☐ Children's books
- ☐ Music
- ☐ Other subjects